"Boyd nails the issue. You ~~...~~ wisdom, and wisdom is wha~~...~~ *Spiritual Life of a Leader* will ~~...~~ ader."

Russ Crosson, author of *What Makes a Leader Great*,
executive vice-chairman, RonaldBlueTrust

"It gives me pleasure to commend *The Spiritual Life of a Leader* by Boyd Bailey, my friend and fellow laborer in the fields of the Lord. My delight comes from the fact that this book proclaims with punch and pith that spiritual leadership is not a matter of tips and techniques, but instead the humble cultivation of the inside-out qualities of the life of Christ mediated by the presence and power of the Spirit of God in the life of the leader. When this interior life is reflected and refracted through the lifestyle, qualities, and practice of the few who trust Jesus enough to take the risks of radical obedience, the world will behold a marvel of God's grace that demands an explanation."

Ken Boa, Reflections Ministries

"Boyd clearly understands that leadership is grounded in our being. Every decision and action ultimately come from who a leader is—heart, soul, and mind. Only when the leader is firmly grounded in a deep, intimate relationship with God can he or she provide the spiritual leadership that is so desperately needed in our world today, especially in the marketplace. *The Spiritual Life of a Leader* provides a practical roadmap for our personal, transformational leadership journey that will result in fulfilling God's purpose for our lives."

Bev Upton Williams, CEO Haggai International

"God placed each of us within His story and on a quest for that which is spiritual. He made us in the image of Himself and desires that we follow His Son. My prayer is that God might use Boyd Bailey and *The Spiritual Life of a Leader* to help you on your quest as you lead others. Knowing Boyd for more than a decade, he lives his quest seeking that which is spiritual, and he shares his learnings here. Enjoy your quest. Boyd, thank you for helping each of us!"

Cliff Robinson, EVP and chief people officer, Chick-fil-A, Inc.

"*The Spiritual Life of a Leader* is a passionate cry from the heart from someone whose wisdom has evolved from walking with his Master Jesus. I have read every book Boyd has written on wisdom. This book stands tall as an accumulation of ideas, insights, and specific directions for spiritual leadership. It's an internship for those who seek to lead spirituality."

Jack McEntee, retired, former CEO of Nth Degree

"This book is Boyd at his best, combining his expertise in leadership with his passion for spiritual formation. It's a book filled with wisdom, guidance, and honesty about the struggles along the way. And Boyd's heart shows through on every page."

Terry Glaspey, author of *Discovering God Through the Arts* and *75 Masterpieces Every Christian Should Know*

"Boyd Bailey is hitting a nail most of us are embarrassed to admit needs hitting and is rampantly operating in most churches. The business of church has swallowed communion with God. Boyd has pulled aside the veil on intimacy and religion to speak life and address the one thing our souls all want more than anything else (whether we admit it or not)...rest. If you are burned out and tired of being a good Christian trying to lead anything, this book is going to set you free. Boyd writes from a place of knowing and practicing the Spirit-led life and provide a clear path on how to receive it."

Rachel Faulkner Brown, executive director, Be Still Ministries

"I am excited for Boyd to be able to pull all of the things he knows and sees in his work into a timely book on spiritual leadership. You might say that it's easy for Boyd to do this in his own life because he works for a Christian organization. Maybe it's a little easier, but my bet is that Boyd would be using these same principles if he were in a secular job. Kudos to Boyd for blessing all of us with this book!"

David B. Plyer, Gleneagles Group

"For the Christian, who is currently, or will be in the future, in a role leading individuals, teams, or entire organizations, *The Spiritual Life of a Leader* illuminates with great discernment the nuances between being 'a leader' and being a God-infused, spiritually energized, empowered leader who is calmly leading above and beyond their naturally given skills and abilities. This book is a game-changer for Christian leaders."

William F. "Woody" Faulk, vice president, Innovation and New Ventures, Chick-fil-A, Inc.

"What happens when all of the knowing and doing still leaves an inner ache within the soul of a leader? This book will guide you to healing that inner ache. *The Spiritual Life of a Leader* speaks to the inner longings that many leaders in this day have avoided or are simply not aware of. Boyd shares openly from his own life what true spiritual maturity is: growing more confident in God's love. You will be first of all healed as you experience God's love on these pages, which will naturally result in Spirit-filled, loving, effective leadership."

Beth Bennett, Mission Increase Atlanta

"When Boyd first told me about the premise of this book, my heart did two laps around the room, a somersault, and then backflipped back into my body before my pulse calmed down. Nuggets of biblical truth, summarized with practical insights shared by powerful servants of God, provide an inside, behind-the-scenes look at the spiritual life and thoughts of a leader. Wow! This book immediately went to the top of my must-read list."

Ron Dunn, CEO Alliance Flooring, and founding director of One Thing for Men Ministry

"Boyd is a wise and masterful guide who takes us on a journey that provides the framework to unleash the leaders God has created us to be. He provides sound biblical counsel and examples of how to strengthen our spiritual lifestyle, spiritual qualities, and spiritual practices that will release the joy of becoming the leader we crave in our soul to become."

Joe Pringle, president, National Christian Foundation Chicago

"*The Spiritual Life of a Leader* is infused with fresh insights. It's inspiring, encouraging, and well-written. You must read this book!"

Angela Correll, author and entrepreneur

"*The Spiritual Life of a Leader* is the litmus test for a life of fruitfulness. Why is Boyd Bailey qualified to write on such a subject? Because he has allowed his Savior, Jesus, to develop him through much trial and challenge for more than four decades. I have been a personal observer of his life of love, empathy, and courage for years, and I'm constantly confronted to focus on God's vision for my life because of his faithfulness in living well."

Matthew Hendley

"During the last year of COVID, as a leader I observed both believers and nonbelievers searching, reflecting, and desiring something deeper. I believe that one of the things almost everyone would agree that they desire of themselves and want from others is consistency. Boyd, who has worked with and walked with many leaders over the years, illustrates how important it is to be consistent in a daily walk through a deeper relationship with Christ. He draws on a wealth of experience that is rich and deep, and he now shares it in *The Spiritual Life of a Leader*. I have no doubt you will be blessed and a blessing to others by taking the time to dive deep into this book."

Jimmy Rousey Stanford

"Boyd Bailey's latest book, *The Spiritual Life of a Leader*, captures the heart and soul of what it means to be a servant leader. In the Foreword, Larry Green challenges us to pray and ask God what he wants us to take away from the book. My answer was clear: to bring my whole heart and faith to every aspect of my leadership. Through each of the three parts, "Spiritual Lifestyle," "Spiritual Qualities," and "Spiritual Practices" of a leader, I experienced a roadmap for a transformational journey on how to bring my *whole self* and *whole heart* to leadership every day and in every circumstance. Well done!"

Eric Storey, Fortune 250 C Suite executive and former Airborne Ranger

"In *The Spiritual Life of a Leader*, Boyd brings biblical leadership principles to life by looking to Jesus as your model for how to lead. Each chapter has a Scripture focus, an engaging life story or application, and ends with action steps to take that will lead to growth in your spiritual life. It's encouraging and inspiring, and it never loses sight of the fundamental truth that being in close relationship with the One who leads best will change you and transform how you lead others."

Rita Felice

"This book is packed full of biblical, practical, and transforming wisdom. The principles and disciplines espoused here will not only make you a better leader, but they will also make you a better person and enhance your relationships in all areas of your life. Boyd Bailey is uniquely qualified to share the wisdom found in this book as he models and lives out these principles in a powerful and compelling way in his own life—fueled by his deep love and passion for God and for people."

Michael King, charitable wealth strategist, National Christian Foundation

"I have had the pleasure to get to know Boyd Bailey as a brother in Christ over the last decade while serving alongside him on various Generosity Events and Initiatives. Whenever we have allowed the Spirit of God to lead us, the burden has been lightened, the fruit has been plentiful, and the joy has been tremendous. In *The Spiritual Life of a Leader*, Boyd shares the importance of allowing the Lord to lead us first and for us to abide in Christ and allow him to work through us. By digging into powerful verses from Scripture, wisdom from the saints before us, and sharing his own spiritual experiences and lessons, Boyd challenges all of us to come closer to the love of Jesus and allow us to be the light of the world."

Greg Winchester, founder and CEO, Summit Investors, LLC

"I couldn't recommend Boyd's latest book, *The Spiritual Life of a Leader*, more highly. It's both timely and timeless! Timely because Christian leaders are under attack by the enemy as never before, and timeless because the wisdom and insights are from our heavenly Father and His Word. Whatever your leadership role, applying the spiritual lifestyle, qualities, and practices in the book will enable you to thrive as a leader, both now and into the future!"

Bill Williams, former CEO, National Christian Foundation

"As someone who has had the opportunity to lead teams in both the private and public sector, *The Spiritual Life of a Leader* is a book I wish I'd had years ago. The concepts, principles, and biblical basis lay the solid foundation any successful leader must have. Most books on the leadership topic cause me to be reflective. This book called me to action with crisp summaries at the end of each chapter that would force me to either reread or write down my learnings and action steps. I am looking forward to using *The Spiritual Life of a Leader* in my current coaching and mentoring activities."

Greg Adams, retired IBM executive
and former COO for the State of Tennessee

"Boyd is one of the wisest people I know. We have been friends in ministry for six years, and I am constantly amazed by his ability to cut to the chase and share truth with love and perspective. His latest look at leadership focuses on the reality that it must be rooted in spiritual growth and maturity. Growing closer to Christ can allow any leader to improve and have greater impact, not just on their organization, but ultimately the kingdom. Thank you, Boyd, for once again sharing your wisdom with us."

David Henriksen, president and CEO, Giving Company

"There is a great focus on leadership in our culture, but the focus on the spiritual life of the leader has been missed by most. Boyd's book is a wonderful, practical roadmap to growth in the most important part of leadership...being a Spirit-filled leader. This book is a great encouragement and a challenge to be the kind of leader that God wants us all to be. You will be blessed by reading it!"

Cliff Benson

"Boyd Bailey has done it again! At a time when so many are searching, Boyd shares the way through his newest book, *The Spiritual Life of a Leader*. He presents God-breathed wisdom to help us become not only more capable, but more gifted spiritual leaders. Boyd shares insights from his personal pursuit of an intimate, vibrant and growing relationship with God. The book outlines in three distinct parts the spiritual lifestyle, the spiritual qualities, and the spiritual practices of a leader so we look more like Jesus day by day."

Kelly Shepard, Love Gives advocate

"In *The Spiritual Life of a Leader*, Boyd Bailey carefully navigates us to that place that still exists and always will exist—the bedrock that is only found in an intimate relationship with the One who created truth, loves us immeasurably, and calls us to both follow Him and lead others to Him. This book challenged me to go deeper and longer in my spiritual journey, and it gave me tools and reminders in how to stay faithful to the very end. This is not a one-and-done self-help read, but rather a rich guidebook full of Scripture and wisdom. *The Spiritual Life of a Leader* is one of Boyd's very best works, and one I plan to share with students I mentor and peers I journey with."

Dan Lewis, founder and president of Next to Lead

"Boyd Bailey is a living example of leading with compassion, humility, and a servant's heart. In *The Spiritual Life of a Leader*, he candidly shares the principles that have profoundly empowered his leadership for more than 40 years. You will be inspired to be a leader who listens for the 'still small voice' and trusts God's wisdom, strength, and, most importantly, love."

Mary Beth Googasian, director of corporate communications,
National Christian Foundation

"*The Spiritual Life of a Leader* is a powerful tool for introspection, a how-to guide for leadership development, and a reminder that love conquers all. In this book, Boyd Bailey challenges readers to take inventory of their spiritual strengths and then details the vital importance of operating in them. The book provides a clear and concise way to identify blind spots in our spiritual armor that leave us vulnerable for attack. With everything that leaders face in society, having a spiritual toolbelt that is flexible enough to provide for quick tune-ups or major repairs is vital. *The Spiritual Life of a Leader* is the solution for leaders at every level."

Kenneth Hill, founder, the Launch Pad Foundation

"Boyd Bailey has been a close and trusted friend for more than two decades. God has used Boyd and his writings to help me grow in my relationship with Jesus, my relationship with my bride, and in leading others. This book, *The Spiritual Life of a Leader*, powerfully revealed to me that the effectiveness of my leadership and influence is directly dependent on my growing and intimate relationship with God. God used this book to help guard my heart and keep me from getting the cart before the horse. I believe this is the most important and needed book Boyd as ever written. This is one of the few books I will need to read regularly to remind me of my highest priority—to love God with all my heart, soul, and mind."

Dan Glaze, relationship manager, National Christian Foundation

"Leadership is not something you turn on when you are at the office, but rather a way of life that is best sustained through a growing spiritual relationship with our Creator. In *The Spiritual Life of a Leader*, Boyd Bailey highlights the spiritual qualities and practices that will help transform you into the leader God destined you to be in all aspects of your life."

Brett Badessa

"*The Spiritual Life of a Leader* is perfectly timed given the daunting challenges confronting our world. In this book, Boyd highlights the principles, characteristics, and spiritual disciplines which, when applied, result in an individual's transformation. This transformation is made possible through an intimate personal relationship with the One who *is* love and wise beyond human comprehension...Jesus Christ. I highly encourage you to read and apply its contents that you may share this love and wisdom with those you're called to serve."

Lee Torrence

"King Solomon said that whoever walks with the wise grows wise. Boyd is one of the most humble, gentle, personable, and wisest leaders I know, and I'm blessed to call him a friend. Walk with him on this journey, and I am confident you will grow spiritually as a leader."

Steve Dahlin, coauthor of *An Exceptional Romance*

"Effective, God-honoring leadership flows from the inside out. When we understand that abiding is more important than striving, we are a vessel that God will use to fulfill our purpose as leaders. Boyd has gifted us with his wisdom as an exemplary abiding leader in *The Spiritual Life of a Leader*. If you desire to become a better leader rooted in your communion with God, this book is a must-read."

Brett Hagler, CEO

"We are all looking for a format or plan to enable our spiritual life and our daily morning quiet time with our Lord to infuse our leadership, our relationships, and our daily interactions with others. With this three-part approach of 'Spiritual Lifestyle,' 'Spiritual Qualities,' and 'Spiritual Practices' of a leader, Boyd Bailey has laid out the format to allow the Spirit to transform your leadership for good! I recommend this book to all my friends, mentors, and advisors in the faith."

Janice C. Worth, president, Anushka Spa, Salon & Cosmedical Centre

"*The Spiritual Life of a Leader* is an empowering, honest book on Spirit-led, wholehearted leadership that focuses on a way of being rather than doing. It's a much-needed challenge to lead out of our relationship with Christ towards others that will transform families, teams, and organizations. I've had the honor to know and work alongside Boyd Bailey for more than 12 years. I have never been in a meeting with Boyd where I didn't feel honored, valued, and celebrated. I've also noticed that everyone else Boyd crosses paths with leaves feeling the same way. He leads from a Christlike, generous heart that overflows with wisdom, kindness, and encouragement."

Ladonna Cingilli, SVP, Generous Giving

"This superb leadership book is written by the rare breed of a consummate practitioner who also understands the underlying theory. By applying a practical biblical understanding of godliness, Boyd fills in the critical gap other leadership books often miss."

Bill Ibsen, co-owner, Relational Values at Work of Georgia

THE SPIRITUAL LIFE OF A LEADER

BOYD BAILEY

HARVEST HOUSE PUBLISHERS
EUGENE, OREGON

Bible translations can be found at the back of the book.

Cover by Studio Gearbox

Interior design by KUHN Design Group

For bulk, special sales, or ministry purchases, please call 1-800-547-8979.
Email: customerservice@hhpbooks.com.

The Spiritual Life of a Leader
Copyright © 2021 by Boyd Bailey
Published by Harvest House Publishers
Eugene, Oregon 97408
www.harvesthousepublishers.com

ISBN 978-0-7369-8245-0 (pbk.)
ISBN 978-0-7369-8246-7 (eBook)

Library of Congress Cataloging-in-Publication Data

Names: Bailey, Boyd, author.
Title: The spiritual life of a leader : a God-centered leadership style /
 Boyd Bailey.
Description: Eugene, Oregon : Harvest House Publishers, [2021] |
Identifiers: LCCN 2020050238 (print) | LCCN 2020050239 (ebook) | ISBN
 9780736982450 (pbk.) | ISBN 9780736982467 (ebook)
Subjects: LCSH: Leadership--Religious aspects--Christianity.
Classification: LCC BV4597.53.L43 B345 2021 (print) | LCC BV4597.53.L43
 (ebook) | DDC 248.8/8--dc23
LC record available at https://lccn.loc.gov/2020050238
LC ebook record available at https://lccn.loc.gov/2020050239

Printed in the United States of America

21 22 23 24 25 26 27 28 29 / BP / 10 9 8 7 6 5 4 3 2 1

For Larry and Jody Green,
who are emptied of self and filled with the Spirit

ACKNOWLEDGMENTS

With deepest gratitude, I thank the Lord for those who have influenced me along the way in my spiritual life:

Formative Years (first ten years)

Pastor Jimmy Taylor taught me to pray on my knees to confess my sins and humbly declare my dependence on the Lord.

High school football coach Richard Ferguson and his wife, Teresa, taught me the Bible in their home, which ignited my heart to reflect and feast on the Word.

During seminary, mentor Jim Sammons and his wife, Faye, modeled for me how to love my wife as Christ loved the church.

Growing Years (next twenty years)

Serving under Charles Stanley and being infected by his prayer life and call for obedience to God.

Serving under Andy Stanley and learning to apply Scripture in how to love others well.

Serving under Howard Dayton and learning how to walk with Jesus Christ in humility of heart.

Maturing Years (last twelve years)

Monk Brother Marcellus, who led me into what it looks like to live in humility, love, and forgiveness with Christ and others.

Our community group, who love me in spite of me: my wife, Rita; Bill and Alison; Andy and Jodi; Josh and Aria; Bill and Betsy; and Jason and Nisae.

Our children: Rebekah and Todd, Rachel and Tripp, Bethany and J.T., Anna and Tyler. And grands: Lily, Hudson, Emmie, Harrison, Charlie, Marshall, Weston, M.J., Wilson, Emerson, and Samuel, for stirring my imagination into a glimpse of how my heavenly Father loves me as His beloved son.

And a big shout out to Terry Glaspey, who with his coaching and editing helped draw from my heart and blend together my love for leaders and my passion for spiritual formations.

CONTENTS

Part Three: The Spiritual Practices of a Leader

FOREWORD

I have been a part of leading the ministries of Cloud Walk and Souly Business for nearly 20 years, and almost every morning I wake up with a passion for God's people to come to know God's love deep within our souls. And for us to learn to live our lives in a humble yet unrestrained way in response to this incalculable love living inside us... all that Jesus will become known for who He really is.

I first met Boyd Bailey about 15 years ago and immediately realized I was in the presence of a man who was living out the same passion for God that was awakening within me. Boyd was alive to God's presence in a joyful, encouraging, unpretentious, and inviting way! A man who knew the true love of God in his heart. A man whose spiritual leadership was born out of his intimate walk with Jesus. A man who is a rare find in this world of ours today.

Since that first meeting, I have found a dear friend who loves and serves God and others like few I have ever known. You will not find an author who holds more concern and hope for the people who are receiving the words he shares with us given to him by God. As you read this book, please know that Boyd cares deeply about you...just as Jesus cares deeply about you.

If you are wondering if this book will unveil what you need to know most in your life about spiritual leadership, perhaps one of these questions will help you decide.

- Do you find yourself in a place where you have a growing desire to become the spiritual leader God has made you to be?

- Do you wonder what are the most important determinants in becoming an exceptional spiritual leader?

- Have you read books on what men or women say are the keys to becoming a true spiritual leader, but your heart is set on knowing what God says?

- Have you asked yourself if your current leadership, in all aspects of your life, reflects the glory of God?

If any of these questions speak to a longing within you, then you may well find the words contained in *The Spiritual Life of a Leader* a gift from above. Out of the depths and intimacy of Boyd's long walk with Jesus comes a rich wisdom of the elements required to become a mature spiritual leader. All the ingredients are here. I would be at a loss to come up with anything else to add. These pages paint a clear picture of what a life that walks closely with God can become.

As you read, Boyd will take you on a journey of discovery and growth as a spiritual leader in a personal, approachable, vulnerable, loving, humble, and yet penetrating way, all the while being guided by God's Word. You will come away knowing the very heart of the author and his Author.

There could not be a better time for Boyd to complete this work. Our homes, churches, country, and world are in great need of spiritual leaders who lead first by following our heavenly Father, just as Jesus did (John 5:19-20).

What is set forth before you will take a lifetime to live out. I pray that this may be a transforming work in your heart, mind, and soul whose fruit will be a blessing to all those who encounter you throughout your life.

I invite you to do one thing before you begin to turn the pages. And it is more important than the prayer I just prayed. Would you pause for just two minutes—just two—and ask this?

God, what is Your prayer for me as I enter into this book?

And then just rest.

Just wait.

Listen for the still small voice.

Listen for His answer.

As your prayer comes to you from God, simply write it down and tuck it inside the front cover.

And then read on as God begins to answer His prayer for you.

Larry Green
A grateful friend of Boyd's

BECOMING THE SPIRITUAL LEADER YOU WANT TO BE

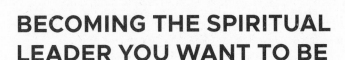

Hundreds of books have been published on how to become a better leader, and new ones can be added to our shelves nearly every month. In fact, I've written a couple of them myself. Most of these books primarily offer techniques and methodologies to help you expand your leadership skills, and many of them can be quite helpful.

But I think most books on leadership miss this truth: you'll become a better leader as you become a better person. The best leaders, I suggest, aren't those who have learned the most tricks and techniques of leadership, or are skilled in "taking charge," or have memorized a bunch of leadership principles. The best leaders have a high level of spiritual maturity—they've learned to walk with God in intimacy and let that relationship spill into their leadership style.

In this book I argue that recognizing your spiritual strengths and being honest about your spiritual struggles are key to your leading effectively. So, then, we'll explore these three areas:

1. the spiritual life necessary for a spiritually mature leader

2. the spiritual qualities that underlie mature leadership

3. the oft-neglected spiritual practices that will help you grow not only as a person but also as a leader

It all starts with our personal transformation, which will change the way we understand our roles as leaders and how we operate in those roles. Whether in businesses, organizations, or churches, we face unique spiritual challenges and temptations others don't have to address. And to meet those challenges and temptations, we must shape our leadership styles with biblical principles and values. We need to embrace the spiritual practices that can help us grow closer to God and thereby become the best leaders we can be.

The bottom line is that spiritually mature leadership begins with an intimate, vibrant, and growing relationship with God. Giving more focus to that primary relationship changes the way we relate in every relationship. Knowing we are well loved by God empowers us to love other people as well, especially those we are called, in whatever context, to lead.

I didn't always understand this principle. While still in my teens, I was already busy learning about leadership and in the process of building a new business. But this was before I became a person of faith. Then as a 19-year-old college freshman, I wanted to date this amazing girl who had caught my eye, but she announced that I had to get her father's permission. *How hard can that be?* I thought. After sizing me up and asking me a few questions, her father told me I would need to attend church with their family if I wanted to date his daughter.

I was pretty apprehensive, with no idea what to expect since I hadn't grown up in a church setting. Would I find this embarrassing? Would people ask me questions I couldn't answer? Would the whole experience be…weird? But I really liked Rita, and I thought I could get some good market research done by hanging around Christians. And any contacts I could get for my business would be a plus! In my mind, then, church was just another useful tool for networking.

Well, I married Rita, and I soon learned that connection with Jesus is much more important than making another business connection.

Even longtime believers sometimes live out a similar disconnect between their "religious" activities and "corporate" ones. In his book *Monday Morning Atheist,* my friend Doug Spada points out that many of us attend church on Sunday so we can check off the spiritual responsibilities on our to-do lists. Then we fail to integrate what we learn or experience there with the activities of our workweeks. Faith makes little or no impact on how we function in our jobs.

Spiritually mature leaders always ask this important question: Where is the Holy Spirit in what we're doing? It's all too easy for board meetings to begin with a token prayer as a tip of the hat to God and then just shift to business without asking what God would want for our organization. I've seen this even in organizations focused on ministry goals, and this leaves those board members busy but barren.

I'm always striving to adopt the attitude voiced by the great eighteenth-century English Anglican evangelist, George Whitefield, who traveled all over the American colonies preaching untold sermons and shared the gospel with millions of people on two continents: "Lord Jesus, I am weary in thy work but not of thy work." I worry that many contemporary leaders are both weary *in* and weary *of* due to their reliance on their own strength and talents rather than learning to lean on God's love, wisdom, and strength. Many such leaders need to not just learn new ways of leading but sit at the feet of the One who is the greatest leader of all.

Through growing spiritually, leaders discover a new focus, a new courage, and a new empathy that will transform their leadership style. And it all starts with having the right focus.

Paul, the great leader of the early church, wrote these words to the Christians in Corinth:

> Therefore we do not lose heart. Though outwardly we are wasting away, yet inwardly we are being renewed day by day. For our light and momentary troubles are achieving for us an eternal glory that far outweighs them all. So we fix our eyes not on what is seen, but on what is unseen, since what is seen is temporary, but what is unseen is eternal (2 Corinthians 4:16-18).

Reflecting on these verses many centuries later, Oswald Chambers had this to say:

The "things not seen" refers not only to the glorious reward and the life yet to be, but to the invisible things in our present life on which our Lord's teaching centers, and on which the afflictions center. So many of us think only of the visible things, whereas the real concentration, the whole dead-set of the life, should be where our Lord put it in the huge nugget of truth which we call the Sermon on the Mount. There our Lord says, in effect, to take no thought for your life; be carefully careless about everything saving one thing, your relationship with God. Naturally, we are apt to be carefully careless about everything saving that one thing.[1]

Spiritually mature leadership means being "carefully careless" about many things in our lives, including our responsibilities, by focusing on the unseen—the spiritual realities that underlie everything else. And the greatest of those unseen realities is the love we experience from God, unseen by our eyes but experienced in our hearts and souls.

Join me as we take a practical look at how this love can be experienced and offered to others in our role as leaders—and how we might learn to lead from a heart of love.

PART ONE

THE SPIRITUAL LIFESTYLE OF A LEADER

CHAPTER 1

PRIORITY ONE
FOR EVERY LEADER

People who aren't spiritual can't receive these truths from God's Spirit. It all sounds foolish to them and they can't understand it, for only those who are spiritual can understand what the Spirit means.

1 CORINTHIANS 2:14 NLT

The delicate and the refined natural man receives not the things of the Spirit of God.

CHARLES SPURGEON

My step-grandfather, N.B. Smith, once said to me, "Boyd, I like my pastor. He's smart and he works hard. But he needs to be more spiritual." I was only a young man in my twenties when he said this, and I was kind of shocked by it. His words sounded a bit judgmental to me. After all, what did he mean by *spiritual*? Did he want someone pretentiously religious, who was self-righteous and looked down his nose at other people? Or a moralistic "stick in the mud"?

Of course, he didn't mean either of those things. He was talking about wanting his pastor to be a little less concerned with all the business of being a "man of the cloth" and a little more concerned with the things of God.

As I've grown older, I've come to understand exactly what N.B. was talking about. It's possible to become so overly familiar with our faith that we drift away from daily dependence on the Holy Spirit, the most necessary thing for understanding and applying the truths of God in our lives and in our leadership. In our familiarity, we can get complacent about our relationship with God and listening to His leading. We can replace seeking an intimate communion with the Trinity with a dependence on our own gifts and talents. We can rely on what we know rather than listening for God's voice.

In our familiarity, we can get complacent about our relationship with God and listening to His leading.

I've always loved the title of the classic book by Henry Blackaby, *Experiencing God*. As he asserts, it's not enough to just *know about* God; we need to be in intimate daily fellowship *with* Him. That's the key to being the kind of leaders who bear fruit in their work. And this doesn't apply to just pastors and spiritual leaders; it also applies to leaders of every kind. Our first priority should be to experience a deep and abiding friendship with God.

Spiritual Receptivity

A hunger within each of us is satisfied only by God, and our openness to Him and our receptivity to His love and leading are the foundation for our spiritual life. Jesus said, "He who has ears, let him hear" (Mark 4:9 ESV). He knew that, before we could really comprehend His teaching, we had to be willing to hear. Spiritual receptivity is born out of an *attitude* of willingness, especially a willingness to listen. Our actions indicate our openness to God's agenda, but they're the result of a posture of wanting to hear.

God is always waiting to enter our hearts, and our gratitude and humility open the door. Then, as we start to pay serious attention to His voice, the Holy Spirit infuses our hearts with insight, and we can live in obedience and bear fruit.

God is always waiting to enter our hearts,
and our gratitude and humility open the door.

As I indicated earlier, a deeper spiritual understanding of the ways of the Lord isn't reserved for pastors and spiritual leaders—or scholars or saints. It's not to be achieved only by a select group of "professional" Christians. It can be achieved by anyone who wants to find it. In fact, sometimes the vocation of ministry can be a stumbling block because we who are called to it sometimes rely on *what* we know rather than on *who* we know. In Matthew 13:15, Jesus refers to those who have callous hearts—the people who cannot see and be healed until they turn to Him, until they become vulnerable to Him. Professional expertise is no replacement for depending on Jesus.

Spiritual receptivity means submitting to the Holy Spirit's prodding in order to preempt my pride. I need to be humble. Instead of just depending on the latest data or how wise and knowledgeable I think I am, I must process everything through prayer. Praying opens up my perspective to see things the way God sees them and to do things the way God would do them.

Spiritual Fervor

Our goal is not to become religious but to become "on fire" for Christ. To be fervent. Spiritual fervor is the evidence of a faith that's alive—vibrant, effervescent, lifegiving, and expectant. It's the contagious commitment that leads others to notice something about our walk with God is different. As Paul encourages, "Never be lacking in zeal, but keep your spiritual fervor, serving the Lord. Be joyful in hope, patient in affliction, faithful in prayer" (Romans 12:11-12).

Spiritual fervor is the evidence of a faith that's alive.

When you're fervent, you lift the spirits of those around you. You point them toward dependence on God as they see the fruit of this characteristic in your life. Just as the flame from a matchstick ignites a fuse on a stick of dynamite, so your spiritual spark can enflame others to seek the spiritual path. You'll become the kind of leader other people want to follow. You'll set an example by the priority you give to prayer, by your generosity, and by your love for the Scriptures. Zeal for Christ is not so much taught as it's caught.

Fervor isn't just an emotional response you drum up within yourself. It's gained by spending time at the feet of Jesus, listening and learning His ways. Reading and studying the Bible is probably the most powerful way you can hear God speak, and applying Scripture to your life will be like pouring gasoline on a campfire. The Bible is explosive, and it makes you combustible for Christ. He brings His Word alive in you.

It isn't enough to be zealous, however. Your fervor should be ignited by the knowledge you gain from studying Scripture and spending time in prayer. Ignorance on fire can be dangerous, damaging relationships and alienating those who might otherwise want to hear about Jesus.

Laziness, when it comes to spiritual learning, is never a virtue, but neither is the kind of overconfident self-righteousness some spiritual leaders exhibit. Such self-righteousness is never appealing or effective in communicating with others. Make it your goal to be a pleasing fragrance in every situation. Second Corinthians 2:15-16 says, "We are to God the pleasing aroma of Christ among those who are being saved and those who are perishing. To the one we are an aroma that brings death; to the other, an aroma that brings life."

Spiritual Training

A couple of years ago I was finally fed up with failing to keep myself physically fit. Nothing I did on my own was working, so I hired a trainer named Don. As I said to him, "Don, I would rather pay you $250 a month than thousands of dollars for an angioplasty."

Don is a pretty impressive specimen because he's spent a number of years focused on stretching, strength training, and eating well. He set up a customized training regimen for me, and it's resulted in my having more stamina and mobility than I'd had in years. But there's been a price for this improvement. When I leave my sessions with him, I'm seriously sore—and not just ibuprofen sore! Don pushes me in the ways I need to be pushed if I want to make progress. And because of the time and effort I've invested, I now have more energy to serve others. Just as important, I have the energy to wrestle on the floor with my grandchildren!

Paul compares living the Christian life to a runner who prepares for a race or a boxer getting ready for a big fight. We must, he says, train just like a successful athlete: "Athletes exercise self-control in all things; they do it to receive a perishable wreath, but we an imperishable one. So I do not run aimlessly, nor do I box as though beating the air" (1 Corinthians 9:25-26 NRSV). In other words, we need to train hard in the spiritual life the same way an athlete must train for a competition. And as with the athlete, it always helps us to know what we're training for and understand the goal we have in mind.

Like the marathon runner, we need a burning desire to win. Otherwise, we may never finish the race. You can't just wake up one day and decide to run the Boston Marathon the next week. You have to work toward it. It's the same with the spiritual race Paul talks about. Without a vision and goal, all our daily practices and habits can easily be misdirected. And we need to know how to reach our goal and fulfill that vision.

So what is the primary goal we're striving to reach as leaders? It's nothing less than embracing a level of communion with God that will ultimately affect the community of people we serve as leaders. It's becoming more loving and Christlike in everything we do.

A clear vision of becoming like Christ will motivate us to engage in the necessary spiritual training. This training involves the way we live each day. Daily, then, we are renewed by God's love as we conform to His plan for us, surrender to His will, and continually make the small choices that keep us on the path toward intimacy with Him. We understand that our life stories aren't just disconnected, meaningless strings of isolated events and situations. They're given meaning as we live in harmony with the stories God wants to tell through us.

Why would we not want to pursue a life of the Lord's ultimate purpose rather than a life of chaos and disappointment?

True Spirituality or False Spirituality

In our day and age, a lot of counterfeit spiritualities call for our attention. They make promises for peace and prosperity without asking for commitment and discipline. Some speak loudly of Christian values yet use their influence to get their own way or prey on the good faith of other believers. Religion can sometimes become part of a leader's personal power trip. Some leaders even use Bible verses and Christian values to control other people or manipulate them into doing what they want them to do. They might, for instance, use a Scripture reference to close a business deal or make a sale.

One of the worst types of spiritual deception is using God to get our own way. In the end, such leaders will learn the lesson of Simon in the early church (Acts 8:17-19): it never works to try to bribe the Holy Spirit or purchase His power for our own ends. This is false spirituality.

One of the worst types of spiritual deception is using God to get our own way.

True spirituality, on the other hand, is motivated and controlled by the Spirit of Christ. God is the initiator. And true spirituality is never focused primarily on us and our desires but measured by how well we serve others. True spirituality is based on integrity and authenticity and obedience rather than on showy religiosity. In the world of leadership, true spirituality is seen in those leaders who focus on becoming a servant.

You might not recognize true spirituality immediately, but its reality becomes evident over time. It's forged on the anvil of adversity, taught at the hearth of humility, and received at the gate of God's grace. True spirituality always begins with the question every leader needs to ask those they lead: "How can I serve you?"

> True spirituality always begins with the
> question every leader needs to ask those
> they lead: "How can I serve you?"

Spiritually Mature Leaders...

- learn to listen for and hear the voice of the Spirit in all their dealings with others,

- spend time sitting at the feet of the Savior to let Him teach them, especially on how to lead,

- pursue a clear spiritual vision for their own life, their ministry, and their business,

- focus on the practical steps necessary to reach their spiritual goals, and

- understand that serving others, including those whom they're called to lead, is the key to true spirituality.

CHAPTER 2

ABIDING AND BEARING FRUIT

Abide in Me, and I in you. As the branch cannot
bear fruit of itself unless it abides in the vine, so
neither can you unless you abide in Me.

JOHN 15:4 NASB

[The believer's] union with his Lord is no work of
human wisdom or human will, but an act of God.

ANDREW MURRAY

When Jesus speaks of abiding, He means dwelling with Him but also dwelling in the company of those you love. This is very much in line with this extended entry Webster's dictionary once offered for the word *abide*:

> In general, *abide* by signifies to adhere to, maintain, defend, or stand to, as to *abide* by a promise, or by a friend; or to suffer the consequences, as to *abide* by the event, that is, to be fixed or permanent in a particular condition.[2]

How well those definitions capture the many meanings of abiding. It means to stay close, to stay loyal, and to stay true.

In his classic book *Abiding in Christ*, Andrew Murray reminds his readers that the work of God's grace places believers in a position of abiding in Christ and remaining in Christ. He writes,

Oh, that you would come and begin simply to listen to His Word and to ask the one question: Does He really mean that I should abide in Him? The answer His Word gives is so simple and so sure: By His almighty grace you now are in Him; that same almighty grace will indeed enable you to abide in Him. By faith you became partakers of the initial grace; by that same faith you can enjoy the continuous grace of abiding in Him.[3]

To have a flourishing spiritual life is not to merely ascribe to a set of doctrines and beliefs but to experience the indwelling power of abiding in Christ. Just as fruit won't grow if removed from the tree that gives it life, so we gain strength by remaining attached to Christ. In John 15:4, Jesus told His disciples, "Remain in me, as I also remain in you. No branch can bear fruit by itself; it must remain in the vine. Neither can you bear fruit unless you remain in me."

Remaining in Him

What does it mean to "remain" in Jesus? For starters, it means you should keep pace with Him—not run ahead of Him or lag behind. Unbridled zeal can send you sideways with what the Spirit wants to accomplish in your life. On the other hand, an unwillingness to make your relationship with Him a priority will cause you to be out of step with His plans for you. You need to abide with Him and remain in Him. God's presence is pregnant with possibilities for the focused and unhurried heart.

God's presence is pregnant with possibilities
for the focused and unhurried heart.

To abide is to be present in His presence—or as the great spiritual writer Brother Lawrence spoke of this experience, to "practice the presence of God." Learning to practice the presence of God will make all the difference in our spiritual lives, giving us a source of strength, power, and wisdom for our spiritual journeys. In humility, we stand in awe of the One who gave us His all.

When we remain at the feet of Jesus, we position ourselves to listen and learn from Him. And through abiding, through practicing His presence, we are changed. We become more like the One we're inviting to be present in every moment of our lives. As 1 John 2:24 instructs us, "See that what you have heard from the beginning remains in you. If it does, you also will remain in the Son and in the Father." Abide in God and He will abide in you!

It can be hard to rest in His presence when friends and colleagues are rushing by on the fast track to building their careers and vigorously pursuing material success. It's difficult to be content to abide in Christ when we worry about what we might be missing by our quiet practice of abiding in Him. Instead, we want action. Rather than staying put and listening for guidance, we want to jump up and get busy. There will be a time for that. But first, we need to be still before God. Without being still, we will never discern His will.

Without being still, we will never discern His will.

An important part of being still and listening is studying and applying the Scriptures to our lives. Reading the Bible is often a passport into God's presence, for we find Him within His Word. Being grounded in Scripture will keep your feet on the solid ground of faith and faithfulness. Dusty Bibles lead to dirty lives, but well-used Bibles lead to lives God can use. We abide, we wait, we listen, and we learn as the Lord teaches us through His Word.

Dusty Bibles lead to dirty lives, but well-used Bibles lead to lives God can use.

If you faithfully abide in Christ, you'll know the love of God not just as a concept but as a lived experience. Jesus said, "If you keep my commands, you will remain in my love, just as I have kept my Father's commands and remain in his love" (John 15:10). Abiding brings the assurance that His love will fill your heart and overflow into every area of your life. You'll find His strength, which settles your soul. And you'll find His peace, which gives you the rest found only in His presence.

As a leader, you can bring what you've learned from abiding in the presence of God into every encounter with those you lead, showing them the fruit that comes from abiding: inner peace, patience, clarity of vision, and walking in step with God.

Sustained Sensitivity

At one of the spiritual retreats I regularly take to keep my life on course, I had the privilege of sitting for an hour with Ed, a man who's been a priest and a monk for 44 years. I wanted to take advantage of the opportunity to hear his heart and listen to his wisdom, so I asked him, "How can I grow in my capacity to receive God's love and extend that love to others?"

He sat quietly for a moment, then gazed upward (I'm sure prayer-fully soliciting heaven's help) before answering, "Sustained sensitivity." He paused, then added, "To grow in your awareness that you are in the presence of God and that God is in your presence."

I nodded, and then he continued. "My favorite book of the Bible is 2 Corinthians, because Paul describes us there as 'earthen vessels.' We are fragile, vulnerable, weak, and easily broken. Nearing the end of his ministry, Paul confesses his weakness, but at this point of vulnerability is where God's grace and power rests."

Ed was pointing to the truth of 2 Corinthians 12:9, which empha-sizes how effectively God works in our weaknesses. If we can be hon-est about our own need for God, we'll find that His presence is exactly what we need. We can develop the sustained sensitivity we need only when we abide in His love.

Weakness Converted to Love

We can grow in our love for God and for others only when we're honest about our weaknesses. As long as we pretend to be confident and strong and capable of going it on our own, we'll never experience the real strength that comes from weakness and honesty and vulnerability toward God. His grace meets us at the intersection of our broken, earthly selves to empower us to love.

> God's grace meets us at the intersection of our broken, earthly selves to empower us to love.

If anyone could have fallen back on the strength of his résumé, it would have been the apostle Paul. He was not only well-educated but had learned a great many lessons in the school of hard knocks. Though he was one of the greatest Christian leaders, as his life neared its close he admitted that what he really needed was not in himself but in the Lord he served. One of the key signs of spiritual maturity is the recognition that we can't do it on our own. We need the Spirit's comfort, the Son's forgiveness, and the Father's love.

What is the status of your "love tank"? Are you full? Down to a quarter of a tank? Or just barely running on fumes? If you're running out of love fuel, you're flirting with a breakdown. You might be able to coast a little longer, but eventually you'll slow to a complete stop. Maybe it's time to pull into your heavenly Father's service station and fill up your tank. When you aren't moving forward in the love and strength of Christ, you'll find yourself assailed by feelings of failure, unworthiness, and being unloved. You need a fresh fill-up that comes from abiding closely with Him.

So let go of a life filled with negative thinking and overwhelming fears. As 1 John 4:18 reminds us, "There is no fear in love." Embrace the love God wants to shower on you, especially as you seek His presence. There, you'll find freedom from fear and discover the peace of perfect love.

Abiding in Prayer

In prayer is where we most profoundly experience what it means to abide in Christ. Sometimes when we try to become quiet and still before God, we may find ourselves squirming with impatience, wishing something was happening. But something *is* happening during these times of silent inaction—God is working.

Too often our prayers are rushed, and our prayer time is like running to catch a train in the subway. We find ourselves out of breath, and everything is a blur. But when we abide in prayer, we breathe the clean air of the Spirit. The goal is not to check off the quiet time box on our list of spiritual duties but to slow down, rest in the Lord, and pay attention.

In this kind of prayer, we find ourselves exhaling the stress and worry and inhaling the energy of God's Spirit within us. We receive spiritual stamina for the journey ahead and are reminded that we need not walk it alone. Jesus will be beside us every step of the way.

In the silence of prayer everything gets reoriented. Our priorities shift and rearrange. Our faith is energized. We're reminded that we are a beloved child of God. His goodness and grace fill us up to overflowing. In prayer, the words of Scripture come alive.

If Christ is the model for our lives, so is He the model for our prayers. From looking at His life, we learn the balance of being and doing. As He traveled around doing good and proclaiming the kingdom, He also took time away by Himself for quiet communion with His heavenly Father. If He made that a priority, how much more should we?

In prayer, we know God for who He is—our creator, who formed us in the womb and fashioned our uniqueness. He knows us best. And He knows what's best for us. We are His. Psalm 100:3 tells us, "Know that the Lord is God. It is he who made us, and we are his; we are his people, the sheep of his pasture."

Prayer is abiding in God's transforming love!

The True Vine

Jesus described Himself as the "true vine" (John 15:1), which means He's the only source of real life. Other "vines" claim to have sustaining strength, but only He can provide what we really need. Only He is our true source of power and strength and clarity. A leader may learn a skill, hone a craft, or develop her gifts, but unless she's attached to the true vine, in the end she will find only exhaustion, frustration, and burnout. We were never meant to go it alone. And when it comes to the important task of leading others, why would we want to depend on our own wisdom and insight when we can draw on God's?

Jesus revealed Himself as the true vine at a time very near to His crucifixion. He understood that the confidence of His disciples would be shaken by the events to come and that fear and doubt would be their natural response. He knew they would need reassurance when they began to question what they believed and what the future held. He knew they would need His strength to make it through what lay ahead.

He also knows the same is true for us today. With struggles looming in our future, we must decide whether we think we have the strength to face them on our own or, more wisely, we'll cling to His strength like a branch clings to the vine on which it grows.

As leaders we must ask ourselves, *Whose vineyard am I going to labor in? My own or that of Christ? Is my ultimate allegiance to myself or some human institution? Or is my allegiance to the One whose intimacy can make all the difference in my life? Will I let Him, the true vine, provide all the nourishment I need, to give love and peace to my thirsty soul? Will I abide in Him? Or will I trust in my own strength?*

The choice you make here is fundamental to what kind of leader you will be.

Spiritually Mature Leaders...

- bring the peace that comes from practicing the presence of God into every encounter with those they lead,

- teach those they lead how to stay in step with God rather than rushing ahead or lagging behind, also demonstrating the value of faithful waiting,

- pursue sustained sensitivity toward God by abiding in His presence,

- make prayer a priority, and

- model a life of dependence on God as the key to fruitfulness in their life.

CHAPTER 3

PUTTING PEOPLE FIRST

Love each other with genuine affection, and
take delight in honoring each other.

ROMANS 12:10 NLT

To care means first of all to empty our own cup
and to allow the other to come close to us.

HENRI NOUWEN

My friend David is a remarkable person. We first met about 25 years ago, and I was immediately struck by his love for Jesus and other people. He doesn't just talk about being a loving person; he puts love into practice—with family, friends, and business associates. And he shows that love to fellow believers and unbelievers alike.

About ten years ago, he approached me with a prayer request. His son, Nathan, had strayed from the faith, and this grieved David deeply. He and I began to pray for Nathan, and while David was saddened by some Nathan's choices, he never stopped loving him unconditionally. His disappointment never diluted his total acceptance and love for his son.

Here's what I learned from years of observing David's prayers and love: when you sincerely and fervently pray for someone, your love and compassion for them deepens and grows stronger.

When you sincerely and fervently pray
for someone, your love and compassion
for them deepens and grows stronger.

Five years ago, David and I started a book group with Nathan and his business partner, reading books that would help us all grow in our leadership skills. We'd get together and discuss what we'd learned. Many of these books were by or about Christian leaders in business, sports, and other occupations. We all learned a lot, and over time I began to see that the seeds of love David had planted through prayer began to take root in his son's life. Our practice of love and vulnerability in the group was also a powerful influence. Nathan recommitted to his trust in Jesus as his Lord and Savior that he experienced as a child. He began to make better choices, including choosing to get help for his alcohol abuse. The change in his life is nothing short of remarkable!

Because David had persistently and selflessly prayed for his son's heart, his own heart grew in love for his prodigal son. Nathan was transformed by the love of his father—and even more by the love of his heavenly Father.

If you want to be a spiritual leader, realize you have the same responsibility for the people who work with you as David had for his son. And spiritual leaders grow in their love for *others* by praying for ways to love them. This is a simple but profound way to become a better leader—engage with those you lead by praying for them!

Spiritual leaders grow in their love for *others*
by praying for ways to love them.

See Jesus in Others

When I don't take the time to care and pray for other people, my entire focus tends to be on their imperfections. But with that kind of focus, I can't have much impact on their lives. Seeing their imperfections as an opportunity to love Jesus through them, though, makes all the difference.

In Matthew 25, Jesus tells His disciples that, when He is again in heaven, He will separate people like sheep on His right and like goats on His left. To the sheep He'll say, "I was hungry and you gave me something to eat, I was thirsty and you gave me something to drink, I was a stranger and you invited me in, I needed clothes and you clothed me, I was sick and you looked after me, I was in prison and you came to visit me" (verses 35-36). And when, confused, the people ask *when* they did those things for Him, He'll tell them, "Whatever you did for one of the least of these brothers and sisters of mine, you did for me" (verse 40).

His conclusion is stunning: those who care for others in practical ways care for Jesus—and they will be blessed. Our acts for "the least of these" show our love for Jesus because we see Jesus in them. Seeing Jesus in others changes the way we view them—no longer as distractions or problems or interruptions but as human beings deserving of our love and care. What we do for others is a direct reflection of how much love we have for Jesus. If we decide to love other people the way we love Jesus, we'll see them through new eyes—eyes of love. Real love sees Jesus in others.

Real love sees Jesus in others.

Perhaps more than anything, prayer is what helps me cross the bridge from annoyance to love. It's not uncommon for me to catch myself thinking poorly about another person, and sometimes I even get angry with someone for their insensitivity toward me or someone I love. But when I start to pray for them, the anger and annoyance begin to melt away. I often begin to see the bigger picture—how their hurts have caused them to act the way they do—and then I can pray for the healing of those hurts rather than stewing on how I think they've offended me.

Prayer is a game changer. It helps me let go of my hang-ups and lift up others' needs. When I pray for people who are hard to love, it becomes hard not to love them!

> When I pray for people who are hard to love, it becomes hard not to love them!

Whom do you find difficult to love? Look at that person through eyes of compassion and concern. Maybe he's stuck in a crazy cycle of hurt from a childhood trauma that fuels his unhealthy emotions. Maybe she feels desperate and misunderstood and unloved, so she acts out in ways that drive others away. When we try to really understand people we find difficult to love, it becomes hard to hold on to our negative feelings about them. As Henri Nouwen wrote,

> To die to our neighbors means to stop judging them, to stop evaluating them, and thus to become free to be compassionate. Compassion can never coexist with judgment because judgment creates the distance, the distinction, which prevents us from really being with the other.[4]

Prayer helps us begin to really understand others and see the best in them.

Celebrate the Recovery of Others

If we're truly grateful for what God has done in our own lives, we'll take the time to celebrate the recovery of others. In the parable of the prodigal son, the father doesn't waste time on rebuking his child, rehashing the past, or laying down rules for the future. No, he celebrates the return: " 'Bring the fattened calf and kill it. Let's have a feast and celebrate. For this son of mine was dead and is alive again; he was lost and is found.' So they began to celebrate" (Luke 15:23-24).

When we see a son or daughter or even a coworker return from the far country of selfish ambition, immoral living, abuse, or addiction—even from a health battle or challenge that might have been caused by their poor choices—our response should not be criticism or withholding affection. Our response should be to throw a party! Recovery calls for celebration. We celebrate good choices and move forward, and we celebrate the faithfulness of God. We give Him glory for the healing He's brought into the lives of the prodigals as well as in our own lives. God is the seeker of the lost. He never gives up on anyone, including those who have given up on Him. That is the example we should follow as we think about how to love those who are difficult to love.

As leaders, we need to especially focus on how we can celebrate the positive steps those we're leading make. We need to pray for them, encourage them, and celebrate every victory in their lives. Spiritual leaders look for excuses to make a big deal over another's progress.

> Spiritual leaders look for excuses to make
> a big deal over another's progress.

Helping Others Help Themselves

One of the best ways you can show love to others is to help those capable of helping themselves if only they knew how and understood the importance of doing so. This is how love can be wedded to dignity, and this is one of the ways we can, as we're told in Philippians 2:4, look to the interests of others.

Three of my longtime friends are great examples of this kind of leadership. They empower employees through helping them develop a strong personal work ethic. Pete, David, and Bob create work environments where dignity and productive work habits come together, and these environments give their employees a sense of pride and accomplishment by fostering responsibility and accountability, all within a context of respect and love.

Of course, some people can help themselves but choose to be lazy. Perhaps that's why, in part, the apostle Paul wrote to the Thessalonians,

> We worked day and night, laboring and toiling so that
> we would not be a burden to any of you. We did this, not
> because we do not have the right to such help, but in order to
> offer ourselves as a model for you to imitate. For even when
> we were with you, we gave you this rule: "The one who is
> unwilling to work shall not eat" (2 Thessalonians 3:8-10).

Paul knew the secret to helping capable people in need was to give them a hand up, not just a handout. Of course, sometimes people need some financial help, but the long-term solution is not in creating a welfare dependence but in encouraging them toward the joy to be found in work and accomplishment. Paul showed the Thessalonians what a diligent and productive work ethic looked like. He sought responsible ways to help people by helping them grow more responsible. The dignity of work brings out the best in everyone and increases everyone's opportunities for success.

Charity has a place, of course, and that's often the first way our love can be shown: by helping people meet their immediate needs. But then we need to help them toward a more abundant life for themselves—physically, spiritually, and financially. Eternal rewards await those who make this a priority.

So how can we start others on this path?

First, we should ask the Lord to break our hearts with the things that break His heart. That includes all the needs people have and all the hopelessness and despair that overwhelms them. Out of our own brokenness, then, we are best able to serve the brokenhearted.

Second, we need to get to know the people suffering and try to understand the circumstances that led to their lack. We need to become a true friend to them.

Third, we can help them assess their assets (gifts and talents, time, experience, and so on) and learn how they can leverage them to move forward.

Last, we can look for businesses and ministries finding success in models for building financial sustainability for the poor and disadvantaged and learn what we can from them.

Leadership is primarily about people, so it demands vulnerability and availability. And it seeks to model those qualities and skills that lead to a successful life.

Leadership is primarily about people, so it demands vulnerability and availability. And it seeks to model those qualities and skills that lead to a successful life.

Spiritually Mature Leaders...

- commit themselves to regular prayer for those they lead,

- remember that loving Jesus is best done through loving people,

- celebrate the victories and recoveries of others, without judgment or criticism,

- help others who are capable learn how to help themselves, and

- see the needs of those they work with as an opportunity for serving them and educating them in the tools they need for success.

CHAPTER 4

THE POWER OF VULNERABILITY

Confess your sins to each other and pray for each other so that you may be healed. The earnest prayer of a righteous person has great power and produces wonderful results.

JAMES 5:16 NLT

No vulnerability, no creativity. No tolerance for failure, no innovation. It is that simple. If you're not willing to fail, you can't innovate. If you're not willing to build a vulnerable culture, you can't create.

BRENÉ BROWN

This past summer I took my annual spiritual retreat at a monastery. It was time to be quiet and listen to God, but mostly I was troubled by the difficulty I was having—trying to love a certain person for whom I couldn't stir up much empathy. He has inflicted great pain on someone I love through his uncontrollable fits of rage, and reflecting on what he'd put my friend through, I could find little more than anger toward him in my heart.

How could I deal with my feelings about this abusive individual? My concentration on the recent events where his ugliness had damaged my friend made it hard to focus on the purpose of this retreat—for me to grow closer to God. I needed some wisdom, so I sought out

Father David, a monk whose every action seemed to reflect God's love. Maybe he could help.

"So," I enquired of him, "how can I love someone who's hard to love, especially a person who's hurt someone very dear to me?"

He thought for a moment, then said, "It's been my experience that chronically angry, even violent individuals have a lot of unresolved pain and hurt in their heart. They're people who haven't yet been healed by the love of God." He paused as he let me take that in, then said, "Your role is to love generously, and it's the Lord's responsibility to heal his heart."

I knew what he was saying was absolutely true. He wasn't justifying the actions of the abuser; he was calling me to practice "hard love." I needed to ask the Spirit to show me *His* love for my enemy. That was a good place to start—prayer.

The Lord brought to mind the story of how the David of the Bible dealt with Saul, whose bitterness had made the younger man the target of his ire and threatened his life. When David had a chance for revenge, to ambush an unsuspecting Saul, he didn't take it. Instead, he recommitted himself to working out the problem. In this passage, he'd just told Saul about his decision not to finish him:

> Saul said, "Can this be the voice of my son David?" and he wept in loud sobs. "You're the one in the right, not me," he continued. "You heaped good on me; I've dumped evil on you. And now you've done it again—treated me generously" (1 Samuel 24:16-17 MSG).

I saw that I needed to be more like David, who set his pursuer free. David extended generosity and respect to the man who saw him as an antagonist. Only this kind of generous love can overcome a greedy, jealous, and hurting heart. Only this kind of generous forgiveness can heal a relationship…and heal a soul.

Generous love originates in our generous God. He is always giving. He gives grace when we don't deserve it. He gives mercy when we don't deserve it. And He gives kindness when we certainly don't deserve it. Most of all, though, He gives His love when we're hard to love. A love that calms our troubled hearts, soothes our stressed spirits, and infuses a supernatural peace in our minds.

Do you sometimes find yourself obsessing about an injury at the hands of an unjust person who's robbed you of joy? If so, the first step is simply to receive God's love in your own heart and accept the shepherding care of Jesus, the lover of your soul. Letting Christ care for your soul with His indiscriminate, intimate, and always available abundance of love will begin to transform the way you look at that other person. It will soften the hardness in your heart. Jesus's example teaches us how to see our perceived enemies the way God sees them—worthy of respect and love and sympathy. He said,

> I tell you, love your enemies. Help and give without expecting a return. You'll never—I promise—regret it. Live out this God-created identity the way our Father lives toward us, generously and graciously, even when we're at our worst. Our Father is kind; you be kind (Luke 6:35-36 MSG).

When your "enemies" are at their most vulnerable, that's when you, as an effective spiritual leader, must choose not to take advantage of their vulnerability. Instead, love them in a way that draws them to the way of Jesus Christ.

Love Asks Vulnerable Questions

Asking the right questions is a key to developing vulnerability in any relationship, whether with your spouse, your children, your friends, or your coworkers. Don't ask questions that intrude or make anyone feel nervous and exposed. Ask the kind of questions that will draw them out of their protective shell so they can reveal what's really going on inside.

Here are three questions Rita and I are attempting to work into our conversations with each other:

1. How did I make you feel loved last week?

2. How can I make you feel loved this week?

3. How can I pray for you?

At first, I struggled with the word *feel*, because feelings can be dangerous, and sharing them even with my wife might reveal more than I want to reveal. But they're key to making connection. If I really want to make progress in building a relationship, I need to give emotions their proper place. And hearing the answers to these three questions tells me what I'm doing right with Rita. She might answer something like, "You made me feel loved when you told me about your day—the good, the bad, and the ugly. I was able to connect with your authentic self." Other times she patiently teaches me what I'm doing wrong. (What I think is working may be totally off the mark!)

You see, asking questions is the key that opens a door to understanding and building healthy relationships. Asking them isn't always easy and efficient, but it is always effective.

> Asking questions is the key that opens a door to understanding and building healthy relationships.

Are feelings your friend? Or are they your enemy?

When you submit your feelings to the Lord and surrender them to His love, you've found a way to be a better friend. Acknowledging your feelings can help you build intimacy and understanding with other people. And when you're honest about your own emotions, others can be more comfortable about being honest with theirs.

So go ahead. Cry when it's appropriate. Show care and affection. When you can, wear your heart on your sleeve. Believe me, this kind of vulnerability will transform your relationships as well as transform you. And most importantly, when you allow yourself to be loved by God, you have a reservoir of love to draw on in loving others.

Ask God questions like these three:

1. Lord, how do You love me right now?

2. Jesus, how do You want me to love those who are hard to love?

3. Father, I feel rejected by a friend. How do You feel about me?

Vulnerability with God makes it easier to be vulnerable with others. When you aren't hiding your faults and failings from Him, you don't have as much need to hide them from people. You can own who you are and more easily overlook the faults of others.

Paul had great advice about this:

> You are always and dearly loved by God! So robe yourself with virtues of God, since you have been divinely chosen to be holy. Be merciful as you endeavor to understand others, and be compassionate, showing kindness toward all. Be gentle and humble, unoffendable in your patience with others (Colossians 3:12 TPT).

Relational Vulnerability

Sometimes it's simpler to love the people you know the least well. The more formal or infrequent the interaction, the more natural it is to see only the "presentable" parts of another person. But it's easy to mistake first impressions for the full expression of who someone is. When a relationship remains on the surface level of polite niceties, it lacks conflict and disagreements but also intimacy and depth. These relationships reveal only our highly curated selves; they are never of meaningful depth.

Real relationships take more focus, more energy, and more commitment. They also involve more risk. But these are the relationships that offer the deepest reward. When we allow someone to see beneath our surface, they see the parts of our personality we're least proud of and the moments we'd never want posted on social media. Letting people see the real us breaks down walls.

Real relationships take more focus, more
energy, and more commitment. They
also involve more risk. But these are the
relationships that offer the deepest reward.

Those we know best are often the victims of our harshest criticism. How quickly we forget our own shortcomings when we focus on those of others. But vulnerability can be the two-way street that opens up the possibility of both parties being honest with each other and looking past each other's faults.

If you want a clear picture of what such a relationship looks like, I recommend a close reading of 1 Corinthians 13. Its extended definition of love is the perfect description of a good relationship. For example, verse 5 says, "[Love] does not dishonor others, is not self-seeking, it is not easily angered, it keeps no record of wrongs."

Being vulnerable, which includes welcoming the brokenness of others, is a way of telling them you're a "safe place." That your presence is where acceptance is offered and defenses go down. That you can be trusted. For any leader, this is the kind of relationship that makes growth and change possible. People who can be honest about where they need to improve are becoming better employees and coworkers. Vulnerability creates a leveling response in relationships, allowing for true communication and less game-playing.

When anyone can be confident that they are "truly known" and loved "as they are," all kinds of possibilities open up for working together in the most productive way.

Spiritually Mature Leaders...

- offer a particularly high level of love and generosity toward those they find the hardest to deal with,

- draw on God's love and acceptance to learn to show love and acceptance toward others,

- learn to ask the kind of questions that invite vulnerability in others,

- are willing to risk vulnerability in their relationships with others, and

- strive to be a "safe place" for honest conversations.

CHAPTER 5

VULNERABILITY
AND HUMILITY

The trouble is with me, for I am all too human, a slave to sin. I don't really understand myself, for I want to do what is right, but I don't do it. Instead, I do what I hate.

ROMANS 7:14-15 NLT

Vulnerability is the birthplace of love, belonging, joy, courage, empathy, and creativity. It is the source of hope, empathy, accountability, and authenticity. If we want greater clarity in our purpose or deeper and more meaningful spiritual lives, vulnerability is the path.

BRENÉ BROWN

David, a good friend of mine, is a pastor. If I told you his full name, I very much doubt you'd recognize it. He isn't a flashy guy, but he's made a huge difference in the lives of countless people. For the last 20 years he's been quietly and faithfully loving his flock and serving the people in his community. He's made hospital visits, officiated at weddings and funerals, done counseling, preached, and taught classes. And he's much loved by his people. Even when he's suffering from his own personal pain, he's always there for those who need him.

In John 10:14, Jesus described Himself as "the Good Shepherd" and said, "I know my sheep and my sheep know me—just as the Father knows me and I know the Father—and I lay down my life for the sheep." What Jesus said about Himself is the perfect description of a great leader. Like Jesus, like my pastor friend David, a good shepherd lays down his life for his sheep.

But not all shepherds are good—or even real shepherds. Some are wolves posing as shepherds, in it for what they can get out of it. Their focus isn't on serving people but on career advancement. They're the ones who run away at the first sign of trouble, never sticking around for the tough times. For them it's all about self. But with every good shepherd, it's all about others. This kind of vulnerable love is a reflection of God's heart, helping people love and be loved. And whether you're the pastor of a church, the CEO of a business, the leader of a team, or serving your family, you can learn to better reflect God's love through your availability and vulnerability.

> Vulnerable love is a reflection of God's
> heart, helping people love and be loved.

Leaders can show vulnerable love in three major ways:

1. *Vulnerable love invests time.* Love can be spelled T-I-M-E. When someone is hurting, vulnerable leaders show up, shut up, and listen up. They aren't in a rush to leave, and they stay present. Giving time to a person trapped in loneliness, for instance, is an investment of love that often flourishes into a deeper relationship. Reassuring words can soothe a soul, offer hope, and show love in a practical way. But this kind of vulnerability takes time. If you want to lead through love, you can't just offer advice and rush out the door. You must invest the time that other person needs.

2. *Vulnerable love earns trust.* You can't claim or demand trust; it must be earned; it must be built. When we break a promise,

we erode trust. But when we follow through on a commitment, especially when that follow-through comes at a cost, we earn the respect of others and learn to respect ourselves. An attitude of faithfulness, even though we may fail from time to time, builds trust. Sometimes, telling the truth may feel irresponsible, too difficult, or not even very wise. But being honest means we can be trusted to be vulnerable, which means we can be relied on no matter which way the wind blows.

3. *Vulnerable love offers truth.* Let's face it—sometimes people don't seem ready to hear the truth about a challenging situation or about themselves. But truth offered from a heart of love can transform a situation or change a life. When truth is wrapped in love, it offers freedom and understanding. And if we tell people only what we think they want to hear, we're doing them no favors. We leave them stunted in their growth and immature in their perspective. But truth offered in love can be a serum against selfishness, and it can help everyone involved become more like Jesus.

Truth offered in love can be a serum against
selfishness, and it can help everyone
involved become more like Jesus.

Vulnerable to God

If we need to learn to be vulnerable with others, we start by being vulnerable to God. After all, He knows what's in our hearts anyway. We can't hide our thoughts and feelings from Him, and He doesn't want us to. Just look at the honesty David showed as he poured out his heart to God in psalms. God wants the same from us.

Learning to vulnerably speak my thoughts aloud to God, revealing what is in my heart and mind in spoken words, has helped me. Whether honestly acknowledging my fear or my anger or my hurt or my confusion, when I speak aloud to Him, I open my heart to receive His grace and healing and guidance. Speaking my thoughts aloud gives me a voice that moves me from the status of victim to the status of freedom. When I confess my thoughts aloud, I am no longer trapped in the echo chamber of the emotions they provoke.

When I confess my thoughts aloud, I am
no longer trapped in the echo chamber
of the emotions they provoke.

Vulnerability teaches us to trust that God cares about all our pain and loss and struggle. He wants to offer hope and healing and strength. But first we must admit how we really feel. That opens the door wide for Him to work inside us, changing us by His love and grace.

Sometimes, we all experience what the biblical character Hannah did when in desperation she prayed for God to give her a son: we want something, but it seems like God isn't listening. Hannah, though, didn't take a causal approach to prayer. "I was pouring out my soul to the LORD," she told Eli the priest after he heard her pleading with God (1 Samuel 1:15).

Whatever your personal struggle might be, an honest and passionate seeking for God is where you need to start. The question is, does your desperation turn you toward God in an attitude of faith, or does it turn you away from Him in fear and hopelessness? Hannah knew the secret was in taking all her thoughts and emotions, her fears and frustrations, her hopelessness and sadness—all of it—to God in prayer. She pressed in and poured out her soul even though she was "deeply troubled" (verse 15). And in His time, God showed Himself faithful, but not until Hannah had been completely honest with Him.

As leaders, we don't always need to have all the answers. But we do need to be vulnerable enough to show those we lead that we care about them—not just as followers or coworkers but as *people*. Effective leaders realize they don't know everything and need wisdom from above to guide others.

Effective leaders realize they don't know everything and need wisdom from above to guide others.

Humility

Because self-aware leaders know they don't know it all, they should always keep a humble attitude with those whom they lead. Pride may seem powerful on the surface, but usually it's just a sign of weakness and insecurity. Pride refuses to deal with our own sins, and it puts our trust in ourselves, which is never a good place for trust. Pretense, anger, and fear all clamor to bear the bitter fruit of pride, but honesty, healing, and love are the fruit of humility.

That's why the apostle Peter tells us we should "clothe" ourselves "with humility toward one another" and "God opposes the proud but shows favor to the humble" (1 Peter 5:5). It's hard to hang on to humility. Mine often has a fast-approaching expiration date. But we must, as Peter suggests, strip away our pride and clothe ourselves with a humble attitude if we want to do God's work in God's way. And if we don't, our pride will catch up to us. As Jesus said, "If you have a lofty opinion of yourself and seek to be honored, you will be humbled. But if you have a modest opinion of yourself and choose to humble yourself, you will be honored" (Matthew 23:12 TPT). Yes, pride will catch up with us if we don't continue to seek humility.

How do we know if we're short on humility, if ours has a fast-approaching expiration date? We can ask ourselves these seven questions and answer them honestly:

- Do I always expect others to serve me, or do I seek to serve others?

- Am I easily hurt and offended, or am I slow to become angry and quick to forgive?

- Am I directive and impatient, or do I listen to people with empathy and kindness?

- Am I quick to give pep talks, or do I recognize a wounded heart and offer comfort?

- Do I strive to succeed no matter the cost to my relationships, or do I embrace the success of others?

- Do I think only of myself, or do I think more of others and the Lord?

- Do I always have to be in control, or can I rest and accept the input of others?

If you're like me, these questions are pretty challenging to your leadership style. But I've found that only "in Christ" can I become the kind of person the second half of these questions point toward. Jesus was the greatest person who ever lived, but He was kind and gentle and humble. Only self-aware leaders surrendered to Christ can qualify to lead in humility!

Spiritual leaders understand that God uses imperfect people to fulfill His perfect will. And they do that through the power of vulnerability and humility.

Spiritual leaders understand that God uses imperfect people to fulfill His perfect will. And they do that through the power of vulnerability and humility.

Brokers for God

A broker serves as a trusted agent in connecting two people so they can do business together. As leaders, we can be brokers for God.

There is no greater joy than to connect someone with the Lover of their soul—Jesus.

My daughter recently used a broker to help her find a home, and this broker worked and prayed to find just the right place. She clearly found joy in helping connect people to their dream home. How much more joy can we find in connecting people to the One who can help fulfill the deepest dreams of their heart and soul?

What a privilege to be a broker for the Lord, each day praying for others and staying connected with their needs and fears and hopes and dreams! Every broker earns a commission, and in the kingdom of God that commission is a growing intimacy with the heart of a love that exceeds all other loves and overflows in joy over seeing hope lighten the burdens of those on the verge of despair.

As we introduce people to God's way, we learn to know Him more deeply and intimately ourselves. Facilitating the faith walk of others helps us find a greater joy in our leadership and more fulfillment in our lives.

Spiritually Mature Leaders...

- invest time, earn trust, and offer truth,

- speak openly and honestly with God and others,

- put aside pride and strive for true humility,

- remember that God can use their imperfections for His purposes, and

- look for ways to connect others to Christ: a prayer, a listening ear, an encouraging gift, a creative idea, or an insightful truth.

CHAPTER 6

BALANCING LEADERSHIP AND LIFE

*Just as the body is dead without breath, so also
is faith dead without good works.*

JAMES 2:26 NLT

*Works follow faith as day follows night, and their source is the
indwelling Holy Spirit working in the depths of our hearts.*

C.S. LEWIS

Sometimes I need a little reminder that my spiritual life doesn't consist of just my personal connection with God and the nice theological and emotional responses I have toward Him. When I start to have this feeling, I listen to the wonderful song "Do Something," written and sung by Matthew West. Every time I hear him cry out to God to do something about the injustice and pain in this world, it revs me up spiritually.

Then, without missing a beat, Matthew says the Lord always reminds him that He *has* done something—He created people like Matthew, and you, and me to take the love of Jesus to a world struggling with poverty and slavery and fear. In other words, we are the very answer to the prayer we're praying when we ask God to do something. We are His hands and feet to bring hope and healing to a lost world.

Start Doing

Rita serves on the board of a wonderful ministry called helloHope, an organization born out of seeing a need and doing something about it. When its founders, Andrew and Mary Beth Thomas, discovered their daughter faced a rare and dangerous medical issue, they felt alone and afraid and helpless, not knowing how to navigate the trauma in front of them. Once their child had finally made it through the struggle and emerged healthy, this compassionate couple began to think and pray about how they might help parents going through a similar challenge. They didn't just feel bad for these other people; they did something for them. Their organization, helloHope, was founded on the goal of helping parents like them know they're loved and aren't alone. Today they provide prayer, nutritious meals, and even a little financial assistance to parents of sick children.

Andrew and Mary Beth could have just been grateful that they were past their own terrible experience, but instead, they decided to not just pray for other parents but do something concrete to make a difference in their lives.

As James 2:18 reminds us, we show our faith by our deeds. Sometimes the hardest thing, though, is taking the first step. Getting started may feel like driving through a traffic jam at the pace of a crawl. We want to get going, but we have to be patient as we move ahead, perhaps a bit slowly at first, in fits and starts. But when we take the first step, our heavenly Father takes it from there. If we will begin, He will work through us.

Sometimes, then, it's all about writing the letter, making the phone call, beginning the conversation, making room in the budget, or putting the date on our calendar. One step of faith today leads to God working wonders tomorrow.

One step of faith today leads to God
working wonders tomorrow.

But we must take that step. What are we waiting for? The perfect timing? A billboard in the sky proclaiming God's call? A heavenly visitation? That's not how God usually gets things done. Whatever is delaying us or providing an excuse for inaction needs to be set aside. Then once we've overcome the inertia of our excuses, God empowers us *as we move*.

Is apathy the problem? That's an enemy of faith. It keeps good people from doing good things. Or maybe you feel inadequate to the task, making you overanalyze the situation. You have an attitude of futility, which says nothing meaningful can really be done. Maybe you lack courage. But if we battle all those things and get going *for God's glory*, He will get done what needs to be done through us.

We show our love to those we lead by our involvement in meeting their needs and addressing their frustrations. Love initiates. Love takes action. Instead of complaining, feeling overwhelmed, or giving up, love offers solutions.

You don't know what tomorrow will bring, so do something today. Get involved. Sure, you have no guarantee of success. But if you seize the moment and follow the heart of God, you can begin the adventure of service.

We can all pray, *God give me the courage to take the first step, and then the next one. I trust You to do Your work of love through me.*

Finding Our Focus

It's all too easy to get out of balance as leaders. Because we know the power of getting things done, sometimes we don't make the best choices in terms of how we let our faith impact our whole lives. One can be a successful leader without necessarily having a "successful" life. Too many people concentrate only on their work and ministry responsibilities and neglect the other parts. We need to make sure we're "doing something" in every area of our lives, including six that are sometimes neglected.

Neglecting Our Families

Yes, my family needs the income I bring in from my pursuits at work. They need me to be a responsible breadwinner. But that isn't all they need. Spouses and children need attention, listening, concrete acts of love, and the connection that comes through our simply hanging out together. Sometimes a simple act—reading a book aloud at bedtime, tossing a football in the backyard, helping with homework, or praying together—is the very thing your family needs from you in that moment. Often, the simplest things make the biggest difference. And the greatest gift of all is time.

Don't become so wrapped up in your work that you miss the joy of being a mom or dad, a husband or wife. When you reach the end of your career, you probably won't say, "I wish I'd put in more hours at work." But once it's too late. you may find yourself saying, "I wish I'd spent more time with my family." So don't wait until it's too late. A strong family life will make you a better leader because you'll learn lessons at home that will transfer to your relationships at work.

Neglecting Our Relationships with Other Believers

At times it might feel like you just can't afford the time to attend church services, Bible studies, or fellowship groups. But the truth is you can't afford not to make these a priority. The writer of the book of Hebrews had this to say: "Not forsaking our meeting together [as believers for worship and instruction], as is the habit of some, but encouraging one another; and all the more [faithfully] as you see the day [of Christ's return] approaching" (Hebrews 10:25 AMP).

We need the support and teaching we get from being with other Christians. They keep us on the right path, challenge us in our wrong behaviors, and provide the encouragement we all need. The truths we learn about relationships, forgiveness, integrity, and unselfishness with fellow believers will help guide us in every area of our lives, including in our work.

Neglecting Generosity

Our heavenly Father is the true owner of everything we possess, and He's given us the assignment of using all these gifts with wisdom and generosity. How we use our money and resources is a great barometer of what we actually believe is most important. We can talk a good talk, but our open-handedness is what reveals what's really in our hearts. That means we should learn to give lavishly from what we've been given, both to our church and to those in need. Our generosity is a sure sign we've made others a priority.

Neglecting Those with Needs

Our actions speak louder than our words. How much of our time and resources are we willing to give to help those less fortunate, to the poor and disadvantaged? The answer is a measure of our own gratitude to God for what we've been given. Just as Jesus multiplied a boy's five loaves of bread and two fish to feed thousands (John 6:1-13), so our gifts are magnified as God puts them to use. These good deeds are faith in action, which is the kind of faith God wants to see in us.

James speaks to this very question:

> Does merely talking about faith indicate that a person really has it? For instance, you come upon an old friend dressed in rags and half-starved and say, "Good morning, friend! Be clothed in Christ! Be filled with the Holy Spirit!" and walk off without providing so much as a coat or a cup of soup—where does that get you? Isn't it obvious that God-talk without God-acts is outrageous nonsense? (James 2:15-17 MSG).

Let's commit to walking out our faith with deeds of love.

Neglecting Prayer

Sometimes we claim we don't pray because we're too busy to pray. But the truth is we're too busy *not* to pray! Prayer keeps us focused on God and the needs and perspectives of others. It's difficult to be rude and dismissive of someone on your prayer list, so it's a good idea to pray for as many of those you lead as you can. Praying for people keeps them at the top of your mind and helps you find God's strength and direction for all your dealings with them.

My affections follow fast after my humble and earnest prayers. And people who know they're being prayed for also gain the perspectives and strength they need.

My affections follow fast after my
humble and earnest prayers.

Neglecting God's Word

To be a great leader, we constantly need the right perspective on ourselves and others. And nothing will help us with that more than reading and studying the Bible. Scripture contains the wisdom we need and the spiritual food that will nourish our souls. It renews our minds and cleanses our hearts.

I've found that memorizing Scripture is very helpful; it puts these riches within reach whenever I need to call on them. And when the Holy Spirit wants to communicate with me in the midst of a difficult situation or conversation, that often comes in the form of bringing these memorized passages to my mind.

To get more of God's Word into your heart, I also recommend listening to Bible passages as you commute to work, exercise, or do chores around the house. Or download some Scripture passages you can print out, then place them where you'll see them.

Let the Word of God transform your heart and mind. Nothing will do more to improve your leadership skills.

Break Down the Barrier

Some of us allow a barrier between our religious duties and our other responsibilities and activities—as though two completely different spheres exist. We need to break down that barrier and let our faith influence everything we do, including in our jobs and vocations.

Work can be a form of worship. Doing what we do well and doing it to the glory of God can make every job-related chore a way of praising God with our hands and feet as well as our lips. If your work is so joyless that you can't find any pleasure in it, perhaps you need to look for different work. But the goal is to seek to serve God with heartfelt gratitude whatever you do. Worship Him through working hard, sharing a smile and a laugh with coworkers, showing appreciation, and treating people with kindness and dignity. All of these acts are ways we can worship through our work and achieve the needed balance between the physical and the spiritual.

Doing what we do well and doing it to
the glory of God can make every job-
related chore a way of praising God with
our hands and feet as well as our lips.

Spiritually Mature Leaders...

- take the first step and trust God to help them take the ones that follow,

- make their family a priority,

- learn to love and live by the Word of God,

- practice generosity in both financial and practical ways, and

- worship through their work.

I recently sat down with Dr. Crawford W. Loritts Jr., who is a nationally known speaker, an author, and the senior pastor of Fellowship Bible Church in Roswell, Georgia. He helped establish churches in Texas and Mississippi and served as associate director of Campus Crusade for Christ. He was also selected to serve on Chick-fil-A's first board of directors in 2015.

We talked about the connection between leadership and the spiritual life, and here are a few excerpts from that fascinating conversation:

> I think there are some foundational, fundamental decisions that a leader needs to make. A leader is someone whom God is entrusting with His assignments in order to get them done. It's not about the top box on an organization chart. Leadership is about stewardship. Not just managing money, but time and relationships. The only reason why you trust a leader is because of his heart relationship with God.

> ———

> I think, fundamentally, all of us as leaders have to make two primary decisions. Number one is that my life is my relationship with Christ. Everything about me is centered on my walk and relationship with Christ. I cannot compartmentalize the Lord. My skill set and things that need to be done, my list of things to do, projects that I'm working

on, etc. Everything about me needs to be touched by the transforming life of the Lord Jesus, so my life and all that I do in life really is about Him. And I think if you make that primary decision, I'm not saying that spiritual disciplines will be easy, but I'm saying that you won't fight the compartmentalization.

And then the second fundamental decision every leader needs to make is whether or not the Bible is going to be a point of reference and the context of my life. If Scripture is not a point of reference, then there will always be a constant struggle, because when I get between a rock and a hard place, I'll run back to Proverbs to get some nugget there; I'll go listen to this tape or read this blog or whatever. However, if I made the decision, as it says in Psalm 1, that my delight is in the law of the Lord, and in His law I will meditate day and night—it means that I have made the decision that what God says in my life is preeminent, and that's the context. Now, again, I'm not saying that it will be easy, but you won't fight the idea of the battle of whether or not it's a priority to you. You've made that decision.

———

What I give my time to, what is first on my agenda, has a way of communicating to myself and everybody else what's primary to me.

———

God does not want our role to become our identity. Our identity is in Jesus and where He is, so the fruit of the Spirit has to be demonstrated on my job, in the boardroom, in that conference room, in that evaluation meeting or whatever it is, as well as at my kids' basketball game and at home when my wife is kind of busting my chops on something I should have done and did not do. But it's never okay for me not to be Christlike.

———

Jesus says you will have fruit, then you will have more fruit, then you will have much fruit. And I take that to mean that the more you spend time in His presence and you abide in His love, His character, His likeness and all that He is begins to dominate my bio, begins to dominate my personal résumé. I begin to look like Him. And it shifts from being driven by duty—we should never be driven by duty—to being driven by relationship.

———

The song of every person that communes with God should be that old hymn, "I need Thee, O I need Thee; every hour I need Thee." And here's the amazing paradox. In the recognition of my neediness, I experience His power and presence. When I cease to feel that, oh man, that's a bad place to be.

———

I happen to be an introvert who loves people, and the experts said I'm a good case study. If the difference between introverts and extroverts has to do with where you get your energy from, I'm an introvert. I love people, I love being around people, I love interacting with people. But honestly, I don't get my energy from that. I get my energy from being alone and reading. And when I speak and travel, I'm about as low maintenance as they come. I don't need the key to the city. I don't need you to show me around. However, for those introverts reading these words right now, we have to be very, very careful. Yeah, keep your own counsel for a while, but it can be a dangerous thing. Everybody loses perspective when they're isolated. Everybody does. And you end up making foolish decisions. When we're hurting, we need to rush to people and let people love us and let people affirm us. And not only when we're hurting, when something wonderful happens. We need the celebration there. We need to be a part of something.

———

Keep in mind there are only three things that you can do that nobody else can do for you: Nobody can walk with God for you but you. You own that. Nobody, if you're married, can be the husband or wife of your spouse but you. You own that. And nobody can be the parent of your children but you. You own that. Everything else you do, somebody can and will do for you. So that helps me to understand I shouldn't let all this other stuff own me.

PART TWO

THE SPIRITUAL QUALITIES OF A LEADER

CHAPTER 7

LOVE GIVES GENEROUSLY

For God so loved the world that he gave...

JOHN 3:16

It's not how much we give but how
much love we put into giving.

MOTHER TERESA

The foundation of great leadership is good character. Our good character qualities will enable us to work with people more effectively because those we lead will find us to be people they can trust and count on. If we lack strong character, our worst tendencies tend to work themselves into our approach to leading others. With strong character, we can draw on resources of caring and integrity and honesty to guide our team down the best path.

In Galatians 5:22, the apostle Paul enumerates nine qualities he labels "the fruit of the Spirit": love, joy, peace, patience, kindness, goodness, faithfulness, gentleness, and self-control. Just looking over the list, we all recognize that we often fall short in many of these areas. And that's why it's important to remember that these character qualities are the fruit of "the Spirit," not the result of our natural tendencies and gifts. Only through our reliance on God's Spirit can we become people of character and leaders of character.

In the next several chapters, we'll explore each fruit of the Spirit, with a special emphasis on how they might help us become better and more effective leaders.

Love Keeps Giving

The first spiritual fruit listed is love, and it's likely first because it's the basis for all the others. Love is the quality that leads us to put the needs of other people before our own, and an effective spiritual leader cares for and serves others with love.

An effective spiritual leader cares
for and serves others with love.

In a previous chapter I talked about my pastor friend, David. He's a perfect example of someone who prioritizes the needs of others over his own needs. He is a good shepherd, one whose life is modeled on Jesus, the ultimate good shepherd. David does everything he can to make sure his flock is cared for, encouraged, guided, and taught. He's always ready to lay aside his own security and convenience for them— a form of laying down his life (John 10:15).

If you're a leader within a company or an organization, follow this same pattern even though, as for David, the personal cost can sometimes be great. Look for ways to meet the personal needs of your people. Always strive to be just and fair. Listen and respect every coworker. Don't focus on what is best for you but on what is best for them.

Love always approaches every situation with an attitude of willingness to give. Let me suggest three areas where love should always keep giving:

1. *Time.* As I suggested in an earlier chapter, the word *love* can also be spelled T-I-M-E. Our time and attention are among the most valuable gifts we can give to someone. In a world where everyone thinks mostly about themselves, love makes

the time to be available to other people, keeping aware of their needs and then seeking to help meet them.

2. *Trust*. Trust is the basis of every strong and growing relationship with any other person. Without mutual trust, it's almost impossible to make a good connection. Normally, someone needs to take the first step. Someone must be the one who initiates the relationship of trust by both being trustworthy and taking the risk of trusting someone else. This can start with you. When you keep your word, you build trust. When you break your promises, you erode trust. When you follow through on a commitment, especially in the face of difficulties, you earn respect and trust. If you are trustworthy, others become confident they can count on you. Trust doesn't develop overnight; it's earned over time. And again, it can start with you.

3. *Truth*. Truth is a gift of love not always cheerfully received. Sometimes, in fact, it's not at all appreciated. But being truthful is an important part of being loving. When wrapped in love, truth offers freedom and understanding, and it moves past all the game-playing that gets in the way of effective communication. When people are told only what they want to hear, they remain stunted in their spiritual, intellectual, emotional, and relational growth.

We owe it to others to be truthful. But love also understands that tone and timbre are important, as well as timing. Truth delivered with wisdom can transform even the most vexing or challenging problems.

Love and Gratitude

Our gratitude toward God will be reflected in our actions toward others. When we consider how He reached out to us in love and forgave us, we should be inspired to treat others in a similar manner. Gratitude for His extraordinary forgiveness should encourage us to offer love generously. We can never repay God for His graciousness toward us, but He doesn't want us to work toward pleasing Him; He just wants us to accept the gift He offers.

In our work as leaders, we shouldn't expect gratitude from our workers, but we should love them and care for their needs without much thought for whether it will be recognized or we will benefit from it. Instead, we should operate from the gratitude we feel toward God and approach others with kindness, respect, and appreciation. What we've been given has come so we can give it to others!

Mary Magdalene poured an expensive jar of oil onto Jesus's feet as a sign of her gratitude (Mark 14:3-8). Mature spiritual leaders anoint their assets with the precious oil of the Lord's lavish love as evidence of their dedication to Him.

Mature spiritual leaders anoint their assets
with the precious oil of the Lord's lavish love
as evidence of their dedication to Him.

Qualified by Love

Not long ago I had the opportunity to visit the Holy Land and walk with Rita in the very places Jesus once walked. Among the sites we visited was the beach where Jesus appeared to His disciples after His resurrection.

In the context of that miraculous meeting, Jesus posed this question to Simon Peter: "Simon son of John, do you love me…" (John 21:15). Peter answered, "Yes, Lord…You know that I love you," and Jesus told him to feed His lambs.

Then Jesus ask Peter again if he loved Him. For the second time, Peter answered yes, and Jesus told him, "Take care of my sheep" (verse 16).

Then Jesus asked once more, "Simon son of John, do you love me?" Verse 17 goes on to say, "Peter was hurt because Jesus asked him the third time, 'Do you love me?' He said, 'Lord, you know all things; you know that I love you.'" And what did Jesus answer? "Feed my sheep."

As I walked along that same beach, I felt Jesus whisper the same question to my soul: "My beloved Boyd, do you love Me?" I teared up, and just as Peter did so many years ago, I responded, *Yes, Lord. You know I do.* And then I understood more clearly than ever that the mutuality of the love between Jesus and me is exactly what qualifies me, as a leader, to feed God's beloved sheep.

My love for the Lord qualifies me to serve on His behalf. He knows right actions follow right affections. It's better for me, in fact, to be prompted by love without professional training than to have an office adorned with framed theological certificates yet lack the motivation of love. And if you truly love Jesus, that, too, is the basis for His calling you to serve and love His children.

Just like for Peter, a public confession of love for Jesus is an essential part of our preparation for service. Thus, we predicate everything on that passionate love connection, and we pray for opportunities to love and serve others. If our attitude toward other people is primarily judgmental and critical, then we're demonstrating that we're treating them with a different standard than our loving Lord applies to us. Only our love qualifies us to help hurting souls.

Love for Jesus helps us stay close to Him when conflict enters our lives or our workplaces. We deny the Lord by keeping silent and stewing in our anger and fear, but as we acknowledge Him, we can process those fears and frustrations in a loving conversation. Our mutual love compels us to express our love in respectful discussions. And as leaders, our best decisions come from taking time to love others through our diverse views.

Love is patient. Our job is to listen carefully and completely to all sides before deciding the best next step.

Love Pursues You

The love of Jesus is relentless in its resolve to bring you into a deeper relationship with God. It doesn't end with a one-time commitment. Instead, love is a way of life. Even when we stray off the path God has for us, He never gives up on us. Nor should we give up on others. We just keep walking the path of love, as Jesus illustrated with this parable:

> Suppose one of you has a hundred sheep and loses one of them. Doesn't he leave the ninety-nine in the open country and go after the lost sheep until he finds it? And when he finds it, he joyfully puts it on his shoulders and goes home. Then he calls his friends and neighbors together and says, "Rejoice with me; I have found my lost sheep." I tell you that in the same way there will be more rejoicing in heaven over one sinner who repents than over ninety-nine righteous persons who do not need to repent (Luke 15:3-7).

This is such a powerful portrait of God's amazing and forgiving love. We'll all occasionally stray from the best path He has for us, but we can all be joyfully welcomed back into the fold. God pursues us because He loves us. So we should pursue the path of loving those we lead—and maybe be willing to take extra time and effort with the seemingly lost sheep for whom we are responsible.

The leader who prioritizes love is the kind of leader who leaves the security of the 99 to help the 1 who's straying from the vision of the organization or has alienated themselves from others. The one who has strayed away, often afraid and alone, unsure and unknown, is the one we must pursue with compassion and return to the fold if at all possible. So be prepared to leave your comfort zone behind and demonstrate the relentless love of God through your actions. And if you happen to be the one who is currently straying, remember that the God of relentless love is pursuing you and wants to help you return with rejoicing.

Remember to prioritize love. It's the one inexhaustible source of meaning and purpose and peace for our lives. As Henri Nouwen wrote,

> I can recognize and claim my own belovedness, and celebrate with my neighbors. Our society thinks economically: "How much love do I give to God, how much to my neighbor, and how much to myself?" But God says, "Give all your love to me, and I will give to you, your neighbor, and yourself." We are not talking here about moral obligations or ethical imperatives. We are talking about the mystical

life. It is the intimate communion with God that reveals to us how to live in the word and act in God's Name.[5]

Spiritually Mature Leaders...

- give the time necessary to get to know others and allow themselves to be known, in the process experiencing rich relationship,

- build trust through dependability,

- love others out of their own gratitude to God,

- find the source of their ability to love in God, and

- relentlessly pursue love for God and love for others.

CHAPTER 8

JOY ENERGIZES EMOTIONAL LIFE

*The LORD is my strength and shield. I trust him with
all my heart. He helps me, and my heart is filled
with joy. I burst out in songs of thanksgiving.*

PSALM 28:7 NLT

*The Lord gives his people perpetual joy when
they walk in obedience to him.*

DWIGHT L. MOODY

M y wife has a nickname coined by the friends who know her best:
they call Rita the "joy bomb." It's hard to think of a greater com-
pliment. As someone who spends every day with her, I can confirm that
this is a perfect description. I've known her since seventh grade, and
I've seen up close what it looks like when a woman knows she's beloved
by her heavenly Father, her parents, her children, and her husband.
Being confident that she's loved makes it that much easier for Rita to
be a "joy bomb" and put her positive emotions in motion!

The apostle Paul had a succinct command for the Christians at
Thessalonica: "Always be joyful" (1 Thessalonians 5:16 NLT). His words
are all the more potent when you consider that they came from a man
who spent time in prison, who often found himself in the middle of

77

church squabbles, and whose life was often in danger because of his work in sharing the gospel. So clearly, being joyful isn't primarily about our circumstances. Joy is a deeper and richer experience than mere happiness, and its foundation is the confidence that comes from knowing God loves us no matter what life throws our way.

The Joyful Leader

Joyful followers of Jesus, like Rita, are fun to be around. They find gladness and enthusiasm in their faith, and they remain stable in the ups and downs of life because they're filled with the Holy Spirit. It's a joy not contingent on circumstances but on Christ alone. Joyful people always seem to have energy to spare, and their uplifting attitude helps them accomplish much as well as helping others to do the same. When joy is embedded in the mental software of a person, it changes everything. Being a joyful leader allows you to inspire others and keep the workplace a positive and fun place to be.

So how can we become more joyful leaders, leaders whose emotions are energized by the Holy Spirit? Here are some suggestions that might help:

Feed on God's Faithfulness

When we feed on God's faithfulness rather than nibble on the meagre morsels of man, we find ourselves satisfied. Only God can satisfy our deepest longings, and knowing this makes us ever more grateful for His care and concern. Knowing He is faithful—that He is with us and will never let us down—gives us the confidence to get through the tough times with a positive attitude of trust.

This trust allows us to be joyful *always*, not just when life is going our way. As Psalm 37:3 tells us, we must "trust in the LORD, and do good; dwell in the land, and feed on His faithfulness" (NKJV).

Learn from the Lord's Discipline

Sometimes God knows the best way to get our attention is through hardship, so He may have uncomfortable lessons to teach us. We should be grateful that He doesn't give up on us. Instead, He continues to be at work on us, making us better people and healing us of the damage done to our souls by our poor choices. "Joyful are those you discipline, LORD" says Psalm 94:12 (NLT).

We don't have to like the process of being "schooled," but if we want to be joyful, it's essential that we keep ourselves open to what God has to teach us. Then when we look back on times of struggle, we'll be able to see that God never gave up on us, always wanting to teach us and bring the joy of real growth.

Rest in God's Refuge

Rest can be the easiest thing for a busy leader to neglect, but it's essential, and we can't do without it. When God rested on the seventh day of creation, He provided a pattern we dare not ignore. Rest renews our energy and helps us gain a fresh perspective on our challenges. When we're exhausted, we tend to be more negative and more quickly critical of ourselves and others. Fatigue can bring out our worst, while a restored body and soul sing praises to God. Finding God's rest helps keep us positive. The protection found by resting in Him allows us to live with gladness and joy, to enjoy heaven's harmony as we engage the world with a joyful heart.

Fatigue can bring out our worst, while a
restored body and soul sing praises to God.

As the psalmist proclaims, "Let all who take refuge in you rejoice; let them sing joyful praises forever. Spread your protection over them, that all who love your name may be filled with joy" (Psalm 5:11 NLT).

Trust Christ to Change Your Mourning into Rejoicing

When we have a heavy heart, the Holy Spirit has an opportunity to lighten our load. All the losses and failures of our lives and our work can easily weigh us down. We can start to mourn our mistakes and grow despairing about our future. But God offers us a different way.

He wants to turn our "mourning into joyful dancing" and "clothe" us with joy (Psalm 30:11 NLT). Our laughter and a lighter attitude toward our challenges can come when we see a larger perspective and allow the Holy Spirit to baptize our souls with His joy.

Celebrate God's Call to Worship

Worship can be one of the quickest ways to transform our mindset. When we worship God, we take our minds off ourselves and our problems and focus our whole being on Him. God seems even bigger as we praise Him—bigger than our limitations, bigger than our failures, and bigger than our problems. When we proclaim His victory, everything changes. And as we worship, we invite His presence into our lives, a presence that is transformational for whatever we face. We don't have to walk our path alone!

Enjoy Your Successes

Don't be afraid to take a proper "victory lap." A godly satisfaction comes from a job well done, and we can celebrate our successes with God. Our fulfilling His calling brings joy to Him and to us. When we work within our giftedness, strengthened by His help, we can work with a glad heart—one overflowing with joy. May the words of the psalmist come true for you and your coworkers: "You will enjoy the fruit of your labor. How joyful and prosperous you will be!" (Psalm 128:2 NLT).

Fear the Lord and Walk in His Ways

Nothing brings greater joy and satisfaction than walking with God. He wants to be your companion through every hour of every day, working alongside you as you attend meetings, answer emails, have difficult conversations with coworkers, and work away at your desk. To "fear" Him means to put Him first and make Him the center of all your activities. Walking in His path isn't burdensome. Joyful obedience, from moment to moment, liberates us and brings the deepest kind of joy.

Learning to Enjoy Your Work Now

Do you enjoy your work? I mean, do you really enjoy it? I'll be honest, some seasons in my work history seemed like a chore. Pure drudgery. The stress affected my health, my emotional state became fragile, and my mental processes seemed foggy much of the time. I looked forward to my workdays as much as I'd look forward to a root canal! Work felt thankless and boring, and sometimes I felt like I was heading down a dead-end road. If I worked harder, I just felt more exhausted.

If your job feels like that, I have good news: you can find more enjoyment at your job even if it isn't the perfect fit.

It's important to remember that God made us to work. The author of Ecclesiastes, thought by many to be wise King Solomon, wrote, "I saw that there is nothing better for men than that they should be happy in their work, for that is what they are here for, and no one can bring them back to life to enjoy what will be in the future, so let them enjoy it now" (Ecclesiastes 3:22 TLB).

Yes, God made us to labor, a blessing to enjoy. Yet although little is as fulfilling as feeling the Lord's pleasure in our work, it can also be our burden to bear. Nothing is more distressing than feeling we're just grinding out a living in fear and frustration. Solomon knew firsthand the wisdom of enjoying work right where he was rather than being deceived into thinking that somewhere in the far-off future, his work would finally pay off or wealth would bring true happiness. God wants us to enjoy our work *now*.

We can also read this from the author of Ecclesiastes: "A person can do nothing better than to eat and drink and find satisfaction in their own toil. This too, I see, is from the hand of God, for without him, who can eat or find enjoyment?" (Ecclesiastes 2:24-25).

Ask yourself this question: *Is my labor led by my love for the Lord, or do I work for the sake of my love of money or some other competing idol?* Without God's will in the center of your motivation, the desire for making money (and more money!) can have a tyrannical power over your life, over your work, over your family, and over your faith. Whatever becomes your primary motivation in working creates your personal "work culture." Your purpose in punching the clock determines how you think about your labor.

A better path I found a number of years ago has made a big difference for me: asking the Lord, *How can my work be fulfilling for You?* In other words, if I look at Jesus as my "employer" and someone I want to please, it's a lot easier to face the tasks in front of me. There is no better boss!

Hard work is a good thing, but it needs to be balanced by time away from it. Take the time to seek a fresh perspective on your job. Embrace the opportunities available to find stillness and quiet away from your work. Ask God to reveal His vocational vision for your life. Don't just settle for a paycheck that takes care of your bills and feeds your family; look for a deeper purpose in what you're doing. Be patient when work seems extra challenging or less fulfilling in some seasons. And pray. Ask God to help you see how you can use your expertise and experience to love and help the people you serve—your employees, customers or clients, or flock.

And if the time comes when you need to change jobs to better serve the Lord, do it with courage and joy and enthusiasm. Dive in!

The Truth About Life

The truth about life, whether in your personal life or your vocation, is this: how you feel will be a series of ups and downs. Probably, some days you'll absolutely love your job. Almost certainly, some days your work will feel like a chore and won't provide much fulfillment. But it's important that, as leaders, we keep an attitude of joy in whatever circumstances we find ourselves—the kind of joy that isn't fake or forced but arises from trust that we're working for and with the God who loves us.

Whatever your position—in a church, organization, or company—your joy can help lift the spirits of the people in your workplace, encourage them to do their best, and help create an environment that makes them want to be there. The path of joy builds morale and encourages teamwork. It also makes work a lot more fun for everyone.

Spiritually Mature Leaders...

- embrace the joy of working first and foremost for God,

- understand that joy can transform a workplace,

- set a positive example for how to overcome obstacles in a constructive way,

- realize that work is a wonderful, God-given gift that provides people with a purpose, and

- trust God to change their mourning into dancing!

CHAPTER 9

PEACE CALMS THE HEART

I am leaving you with a gift—peace of mind and heart. And the peace I give is a gift the world cannot give. So don't be troubled or afraid.

JOHN 14:27 NLT

Only a peaceful heart can overcome a tired body and heavy mind.

VISHAL SINGH

In a world filled with division, argumentation, and aggression, it's increasingly hard to find people willing to listen and learn, as well as people who will be patient enough to hear things out and search for solutions. Instead, everyone seems to want to just go to their own corner and fight about how to get things done. Instead of raising their hands to ask a question, they raise their voices or even their fists.

We desperately need people who know how to "take it down a notch" rather than just argue more loudly. We need peacemakers. Jesus said, "Blessed are the peacemakers" (Matthew 5:9), and perhaps that's truer now than ever before.

An effective spiritual leader knows how to be an instrument of God's peace. In our time, we tend to think of peace as the absence of conflict, such as after a war or at the conclusion of some argument. But in a biblical sense, true peace isn't just the absence of conflict but a presence that brings healing and draws people together. It's a form of blessing, which Jesus explained in Luke 10:5-6: "When you enter a house, first say, 'Peace to this house.' If someone who promotes peace is there, your peace will rest on them; if not, it will return to you."

Note that it takes at least two people to create a place of peace; our peace alone won't do it. As the Prince of Peace, though, Jesus changes the atmosphere every time He walks into a house or room. And when those of us who know Him enter a house, a room, a conversation, or a conflict, we should be that same kind of influence. Like His, our presence should make a difference, a difference that makes it easier for people to listen, learn, and work together in an agreeable manner. Easier for them to "promote peace" as well. But before you do great things for God and His kingdom, or even make an impact on your workplace or organization, you must live a life filled with the peace and presence of Jesus.

> Before you do great things for God and His kingdom, or even make an impact on your workplace or organization, you must live a life filled with the peace and presence of Jesus.

One of the most beloved prayers of all time is commonly attributed to Saint Francis of Assisi. In this prayer, he asked God to make him an instrument of His peace and provided a glimpse of what a significant impact we can have if we are all people of peace—true peacemakers.

> Lord, make me an instrument of Your peace:
> Where there is hatred, let me sow love;
> Where there is injury, pardon;
> Where there is doubt, faith;
> Where there is despair, hope;
> Where there is darkness, light;
> And where there is sadness, joy.

O divine Master, grant that I may not so much seek
    to be consoled as to console;
To be understood, as to understand;
To be loved, as to love;
For it is in giving that we receive,
It is in pardoning that we are pardoned,
And it is in dying that we are born to eternal life.
Amen.

This prayer, of course, can be a good measure for how well we're doing as followers of Christ. But for leaders, it's an especially good checklist for how effectively we're functioning as peacemakers and thereby positively impacting the lives of everyone in our orbit—our family and those in our workplace, our organization, our church. It offers a great portrait of spiritual leadership and shows how peacemaking can change everything. Since all these qualities can be found in Jesus, the more time we spend in intimate fellowship with Him, the more they will rub off on us and the more we will be the kind of peacemakers Francis prayed he would be. The very presence of Jesus is a place of peace, so He is the source from which we draw what we need in our journey to become leaders who are peacemakers.

Every day a new conflict seems to emerge in the world—a new act of violence or a new issue on which people are unwilling to engage in meaningful discussion. Into the midst of this chaos, Jesus sends His followers out as ambassadors of His kingdom of peace. We are given a message about a different way of living and a different way of relating. We're sent like "lambs among wolves" (Luke 10:3), but we are lambs protected by the Good Shepherd, Jesus. Therefore, we're lambs who do not shrink back from conflict. We're roaring lambs who go forth boldly into the world as instruments of God's peace.

In John 14:27, Jesus tells His disciples that peace is theirs for the taking: "Peace I leave with you; my peace I give you." It's also ours for the taking. He's already held it out for us if only we will grasp it. And if you want to bring His peace into the world around you, these four things can help you do that:

1. *Choose to believe in the fullness of God's love.* We not only embrace Christ as Savior and Lord but as Friend, Comforter, and Confidant. We know He will never leave us or forsake us, and He'll always be with us no matter what happens. Peace is founded on knowing Him, and His love helps us know who we are and to whom we belong. We are beloved children of a loving Father. Whatever stress and turmoil swirl around us, we are safe in His arms. We know peace.

2. *Don't look to the world for validation.* We don't have to prove our worth, for our worth is founded in our connection with Jesus. We don't have to grasp at fleshly things, trying to fill our hearts or gain security, for our hope is based on what Christ thinks of us. The world can never bring us real interior peace. That comes only through the love of the One who dwells in our hearts. So pursuing validation elsewhere is pure foolishness.

3. *Be acquainted with trust.* Trust and peace go together like peas and carrots. In fact, you'll never find peace without trust. When trust is absent, there is no peace. And as children of God who experience peace know, trust doesn't just happen; it comes as a result of the choice we make every day to focus on the truth and rest in the fact that we are loved by the God who is always in control.

4. *Know how to surrender to God's plan.* When we strive to get our own way and fulfill our own agenda, life will always have a large element of struggle. But when instead we surrender to God's agenda for us, we can live in a different way—the way of settled peace. Surrender isn't so much about giving up as it's about giving in. When we lay aside our plans and trust God's will for our future, we experience peace.

Again, in John 14:27, Jesus said, "My peace I give you." Will we accept the peace He offers? Or will we live as though we're on our own—as though our well-being is up to our personal intelligence, emotional health, talents, and skills? When we choose peace, it means we're putting our reliance on Him rather than on ourselves. As Peter recommended, "Cast all your anxiety on him because he cares for you" (1 Peter 5:7).

Who Is the Peacemaker?

If you want to consider the extent to which you are a peacemaker in all the spheres of your life, consider these six indicators, several outlined by Shana Schutte on my blog, *Wisdom Hunters*.[6]

1. *Peacemakers seek to be the first to forgive.* They don't wait for the other person or the offending party to say "I'm sorry" before they extend grace.

2. *Peacemakers focus on their own responsibility in peacemaking.* While peacemakers may understand what others have done wrong, that isn't their focus. They aren't quick to point a finger in judgment. Instead, they seek to glorify God by taking responsibility for their own actions. This requires a humility sorely lacking in many leaders.

3. *Peacemakers know a blessing is in peacemaking.* Though they recognize it might not come immediately, or even in this life, peacemakers know God honors and rewards those who take the first step to make things right. They know that someday, when they're face-to-face with Jesus, they'll hear the commendation, "Well done, good and faithful servant."

4. *Peacemakers understand the difference between peacemaking and peacekeeping.* Peacemakers aren't afraid to speak the truth in love when the situation calls for it, but they're wise about when to speak and when to keep silent. The peace*keeper* might have a tendency to gloss over and ignore the real issues, but the peace*maker* knows peace without truth isn't really peace. Peacemaking isn't about overlooking problems or acting like everything is perfect when it isn't. Peacemakers

bring change through loving courage. They move into conflicts with a heart of reconciliation.

5. *Peacemakers aren't puffed up with pride, demanding to be heard, believing they're right and seeking justice.* Neither are peacemakers wallflowers who shrink back in fear while trying to maintain a false sense of peace—a peace not really worth keeping. They operate from inner strength and are guarded by humility. They want to see love win the day.

6. *Peacemakers don't unnecessarily rush into conflict, thereby creating more problems.* Peacemakers realize they aren't God and can't fix everything. They don't stir the pot to try to bring issues to the surface. They don't gossip, but they will talk with the people involved in the conflict at hand. They understand the danger of operating with assumptions that haven't been verified. They take the time to hear all sides and then have the hard conversations only when they think others are ready to hear.

> Peacemakers realize they aren't
> God and can't fix everything.

Relational Peacemaking

No peacemaking is harder yet more essential than relational peacemaking—helping divided people come together in love and unity and understanding. As leaders, this is one of the most important skills to master. We must learn how to deal with the people for whom we're responsible, especially those who are more of a challenge to us. And we should, whenever possible, seek resolution.

Resolution brings relief to everyone involved. Without resolution, the "disconnect" and turmoil will remain, and this leads to distrust.

Unresolved conflicts are like burdens we continue to struggle under until we can finally lay them down. It's all too easy to fake a resolution and not really solve the problem. In my experience, Christians are often especially guilty of forcing a phony smile when they're internally frowning. Until problems are out in the open, it's almost impossible to deal with them.

It's also easier to talk *about* someone than to talk *with* them. Talking about them solves nothing. If someone remains unaware of their fault, thinking everything is okay, then nothing changes. The way of Christ requires the courage of conversation, so that behaviors can be corrected and relationships made whole again. The unspoken issues will sink a relationship like a hidden iceberg can sink a ship.

Resolution takes time. If you need resolution between you and another person, you must be willing to revisit issues, listen, clarify, forgive, and then reconcile. And it requires humility above all else. Your own honesty and vulnerability are critical for a healing conversation. So, with all gentleness, strive to make peace. Hear out the other person. Really listen to their perspective and their concerns. Make them feel comfortable and not judged. The point is never to prove yourself right but rather to prove yourself to be loving and caring.

Treat others as you would like to be treated (Matthew 7:12). You can't force someone to reconcile. You can't make them see things as they really are if they want to stew in their own resentments. But you can create an environment of acceptance and understanding. Usually, a peacemaker must make the first step.

Spiritually Mature Leaders...

- offer themselves to God as an instrument of peace,
- understand the power of compassionate and empathetic listening,
- know inner peace through their own relationship with God,
- are peace*makers*, not just peace*keepers*, and
- learn the skills needed for reconciliation.

CHAPTER 10

PATIENCE WAITS
ON GOD'S BEST

Finishing is better than starting. Patience is better than pride.

ECCLESIASTES 7:8 NLT

*Most men pursue pleasure with such breathless
haste that they hurry past it.*

SØREN KIERKEGAARD

Being patient is never easy. I have to admit that I get impatient even when I wait in my car at an intersection, thinking the traffic light is taking way too long to turn green. When there's no traffic coming in either direction, it can be such a temptation to just go ahead and ignore the traffic signal. Instead, I wait, sometimes quietly furious at that inanimate traffic light. Yet compared to the patience required in other situations, waiting there is a breeze.

Waiting for the light to change requires a kind of passive endurance, but I'm learning that God wants to teach me a more active endurance. He wants me to learn to slow down, take my time, and not always fight with what's in front of me. He wants me to learn to be patient, and that involves understanding that His timing is always perfect. The tension between trusting and tenacity keeps my heart humble and my will submitted to Jesus Christ.

The tension between trusting and
tenacity keeps my heart humble and
my will submitted to Jesus Christ.

The apostle James understood the importance of patience in the Christian life and how essential it is for getting through life's challenges: "When the way is rough, your patience has a chance to grow. So let it grow, and don't try to squirm out of your problems. For when your patience is finally in full bloom, then you will be ready for anything, strong in character, full and complete" (James 1:3-4 TLB).

James wrote to a group of fellow Jesus followers who were a minority community living among a pagan majority and often finding themselves the target of persecution. He believed the trials we face as believers reveal the genuineness of our faith, just as an exam exposes how well students understand the material they've studied. The life tests we face reveal the depth and reality of our relationship with Christ. When we have a growing faith, we can see the problems in our path as an opportunity to develop a more complete character and deepen our trust in God. We learn to not just passively *endure* but to actively *persevere* through every challenge.

What kind of problems are you facing that invite you into a more patient faith? Financial hurdles? Relational misunderstandings? Health issues? Uncertainty about the future? Unexpected and unwanted changes? Through faith, you can find a new perspective on all these challenges. You can come to understand that when your pain is channeled into patience, it grows your capacity for grace. Otherwise, you'll simply waste the opportunity pain presents. Your pain remains unredeemed, and your wounds fail to heal.

If we want to practice active perseverance rather than passive endurance, we need to be prepared to do God's will in every situation and accept His perfect timing. Our best may still be around the corner, but we can embrace the period of waiting as a period of growth. As leaders, this means learning to be patient with situations and opportunities that unfold more slowly than we'd like and being patient with the people who never seem to be on the same page or the same schedule as we are.

Active perseverance also means we don't run from our responsibilities when things get hard. We don't give up. We keep working with that employee who still hasn't improved as quickly as we'd like, we keep having the hard conversations that lead to growth, and we keep being generous with our time and attention. Even if it takes time, these things will pay off. Patience is a product of continuing hope.

If we want to practice active perseverance
rather than passive endurance, we need
to be prepared to do God's will in every
situation and accept His perfect timing.

Waiting on God's Best

We live in a time of instant gratification. We want everything at the whim of our desires to happen quickly. Our whole culture is based on eliminating the need to wait or at least drastically reducing it. Why slow cook a meal for hours when you can microwave it in less than ten minutes? Well, if you compare the taste of the two meals, you'll certainly conclude that a slow roasted ham or chicken is worth the wait. And it's the same way in the spiritual life. The best things—like growth in maturity and learning how to relate to people in a Christlike way—take time to develop within us.

So we shouldn't think of spiritual waiting as the experience of flipping through outdated magazines in the doctor's office while you keep checking your phone. Instead, spiritual waiting is akin to the waiting farmers do. They plant seeds, and then much of their lives is spent in eager anticipation of the day they can gather their crops. They invest time in fertilizing, preparing the soil, and watering and weeding for months and months, and then one day the full harvest does come in. And oh, is it worth the wait! It's no wonder Jesus frequently used agricultural imagery to help us understand the spiritual life (for example, when He told a parable about a mustard seed in Matthew 13:31).

We all need to find the healthy balance between the active life and the contemplative life. We can spend time actively serving others, giving them a glimpse of God's kingdom in action, and we can also spend time alone with God, waiting at His feet in stillness and silence and enjoying His presence as we await our next assignment. Time waiting on God is never time wasted. This truth is even more essential for leaders, who need to learn to wait before God even in the midst of doing their business.

> We all need to find the healthy balance between
> the active life and the contemplative life.

Patience Diffuses Anger

Sometimes anger is justified. But one of the most damaging tendencies we have in our relationships is to let the natural emotion of anger grow and then push us into losing our temper. Anger expressed this way causes us to utter things we regret, which inevitably makes any problem even worse. Losing our temper never solves anything. It often comes from our impatience; we get frustrated, and then we lash out. Things spiral down from there. We lose perspective, we lose trust, and we invite insecurity.

But if we employ patience when we feel such destructive anger coming on—sometimes very quickly—we can diffuse it and find a better way to communicate. As Proverbs 15:18 tells us, "A quick-tempered person stirs up dissension, but one who is slow to anger calms a quarrel" (NET).

Anger stirs up; patience calms down.

Anger has an axe to grind; patience smooths over offenses and disagreements.

Anger reacts in the moment; patience takes the time needed to process.

Anger rejects; patience accepts.

Anger seeks revenge; patience offers forgiveness.

The goal of anger is to win the argument. The goal of patience is to heal the relationship.

When we learn to be patient, we speak differently to those in our orbit. As Proverbs says, "Patient persistence pierces through indifference; gentle speech breaks down rigid defenses" (Proverbs 25:15 MSG). Patience is a peacemaker. It carries the buckets of water that can douse the flames of fury. It knows how to convene calm conversations rather than indulging in outbursts of indignation. Patience takes the longer view, which is God's view. It helps us calm even the tensest situation.

Prayer provides a good education in patience. In prayer, God waits with us as we wait with Him. And we know that most of our prayers do not receive the immediate answers we'd like. Instead, we're taught the patience needed—a patience whose foundation is trust. God will come through for us, just usually not in our preferred time frame! Psalm 37:7 says, "Be still in the presence of the LORD, and wait patiently for him to act" (NLT).

Discretion and Patience

When I better understand others' predicament, it helps me be patient with them. Everyone's backstory helps explain how they react in certain situations, and sometimes even the simplest explanations let us understand how another person behaves or responds.

When my friend shows up late for a breakfast appointment, I learn his wife needed him to drop off the children at school, so I extend grace. Or when one of my employees isn't producing quite as much work as before, it helps to learn that she's dealing with severe depression after the death of a loved one. Patience grows with empathy and graciousness toward others.

As Patrick Morley reminds us men, "Most marriage problems would disappear if we would simply [patiently] speak to our wives with the same kindness, courtesy, forethought, and respect with which we speak to our coworkers."[7] And if we don't speak to our coworkers that way, it just shows that we haven't learned to listen to their backstories.

If we learn to love people despite their imperfections, we can help them grow closer to perfection.

If we learn to love people despite
their imperfections, we can help
them grow closer to perfection.

Patience gives the benefit of the doubt and doesn't rush to judgment. It takes the time to hear the whole story. Wisdom is found in waiting. "Do you see someone who speaks in haste?" asks the writer of Proverbs. "There is more hope for a fool than for them" (Proverbs 29:20). A rash response always results in messy consequences. But it takes little effort to assume the best, and that usually has the most positive consequences.

Discretion always takes the time to hear all sides before it weighs in with its opinion. The one who listens carefully earns a hearing for their own words. They extract all the necessary information and evidence instead of just offering an emotional response. Proverbs 2:11 promises that "discretion will protect you," and so often I've learned that lesson in my dealings with the people I lead.

Love is patient. It's the universal language that helps those languishing in their faith, and effective leadership requires that we develop more patience.

Spiritually Mature Leaders...

- know the difference between passive endurance and active perseverance,
- understand the spiritual value of waiting,
- strive to balance the active life and the contemplative life,
- diffuse anger with patience, and
- learn to look past imperfections and see the potential in people.

CHAPTER 11

KINDNESS RESPECTS EVERYONE

Be kind to each other, tenderhearted, forgiving one another, just as God through Christ has forgiven you.

EPHESIANS 4:32 NLT

Constant kindness can accomplish much. As the sun makes ice melt, kindness causes misunderstanding, mistrust, and hostility to evaporate.

ALBERT SCHWEITZER

If you've spent any time on social media lately, you know kindness is a character quality that seems to be in short supply. Perhaps the relative anonymity inspires the vitriol people spew. They might be kind and considerate if you met them in person, but forums like Facebook and Twitter seem to bring out the dark side in them. And all of us too often tend to respond in kind when we're attacked.

Our goal as Christ followers and leaders, however, should be to respond in kindness, not in kind. Proverbs 11:17 says, "Those who are kind benefit themselves, but the cruel bring ruin on themselves." In other words, being kind to others is actually beneficial for us.

Respond in kindness, not in kind.

When I'm threatened by someone's predatory attack, I tend to become like a porcupine—I bristle at the disrespect and disapproval coming my way. My blood pressure elevates, and harsh words gather in my mind. I'm ready to pounce. But I've learned to immediately ask for God's help in prayer. I pause and remind myself that He wants me to practice kindness in my relationships, and then when I do, I find my level of irritation starting to decrease. Prayer buys me the time I need to rethink and reconsider the situation, finding the best way to respond.

As Proverbs 11:17 reminds us, kindness leads to restoration in our souls and in our relationships with others, while cruelty just brings ruin. A nasty response to a family member or coworker never achieves anything positive. We may have "blown off a little steam," but in the process we likely scalded someone's heart. Kindness builds people up, while cruel words tear down. Kindness frees us up for real discussions, while cruel words close down the possibility of truly understanding one another. Kindness nourishes relationships, while cruelty starves them. Kindness infuses life, while cruelty brings the stench of death.

In the moment we have the opportunity to choose how to respond, kindness is always the better and wiser choice. It's all too easy for our pride to get in the way and cause us to want to score points against other people, but the one who chooses kindness opens the door for continued conversation.

Kindness is a crucial quality for anyone in a position where they're leading people. Kindness offers and then earns respect, loyalty, and mutual understanding. This is why Paul gave this instruction to Timothy: "The Lord's servant must not be quarrelsome but must be kind to everyone, able to teach, not resentful" (2 Timothy 2:24).

Do you find yourself tempted to react in kind when someone has been unkind to you? If so, pause before you say something you'll likely regret. Put yourself in the shoes of the other person—someone whose unkindness may actually be an unconscious cry for help. Ask the Lord, *What is the source of this person's pain?* Then invite the Spirit to teach you to be a more selfless listener and a more silent comforter.

Show your vulnerability, being gentle and rational, not defensive and demanding. In your conversation, be more like experienced dancers who know they must trust their partners to move smoothly in time to the music. Sometimes your words might feel clunky and unsure, like dancing with two left feet. But with a little patience, you'll find love illuminates the best steps toward intimate dialogue.

Jesus Himself is the great mediator, and we can draw on His strength and wisdom as we try to mediate unkind interactions. We need the kindness of Christ in the face of conflict, especially when we're the one who must exercise the role of mediator. When a nasty response calls forth a similar reaction, kindness has a way of defusing conflicts and actually changing minds. Kindness can even lead to repentance (Romans 2:4). Therefore, as leaders, a caring attitude and kind words can make all the difference in solving relational problems.

Kindness Is Proactive, Not Passive

Kindness isn't just a way of responding to the unkindness of others. It should be on the agenda for seeing life in a new way. In the book *My Door Is Always Open*, created with interviews writer Antonio Spadrado conducted with Pope Francis, the pope talked about how the role of Christians in the modern world is similar to that of a field hospital:

> I see clearly…what the Church needs most today, and it is the ability to heal wounds and to warm the hearts of the faithful, together with closeness, and proximity. I see the Church as a field hospital after battle. It is useless to ask a seriously injured person if he has high cholesterol and about the level of his blood sugars! You have to heal his wounds. Then we can talk about everything else. Heal the wounds, heal the wounds…And you have to start from the ground up.[8]

What Pope Francis is calling for is a proactive kindness, a kindness in action. This sort of kindness steps into life's battles not as a combatant but as a healer. The pope isn't talking about the church being a stationary hospital, which awaits the sick, but a hospital on the move, going where the action is and taking the healing love of Jesus with it. We shouldn't wait for someone in need to stumble through our doors; we should instead carry hope and healing wherever we go. "Be kind," says the wise old saying, "for everyone you meet is fighting a hard battle." All around us the battles are raging, and kindness is one of the best weapons we have to help others in their struggles.

All around us the battles are raging, and
kindness is one of the best weapons we
have to help others in their struggles.

Nor is kindness just about being nice. It isn't just avoiding being rude or harsh to those who cross our path. It's intentional, going forth in the name of Jesus. Kind people sacrificially give their lives away to those who seem to be losing personal battles. We carry the love Jesus gives us and offer it to them. We serve and do not seek to be served as we wade into the conflicts swirling around us. We practice proactive kindness boldly, entering places of chaos and fear and hurt, trusting that God goes with us and before us!

The Benefits of Kindness

Kindness is the great transformer of awkward, negative, painful, and puzzling situations. It brings joy to the one who offers it and peace to the one who receives it. It offers dignity and respect and caring in the places they're needed most. And when someone is unkind to us, we can choose to be offended, or, with a gracious heart, we can choose to take the high ground of humility and gentleness. Kindheartedness facilitates respect as it treats others with dignity and honor.

Kindheartedness facilitates respect as it
treats others with dignity and honor.

At its core, kindness is a reflection of Christ Himself. We can count on the kindness of God. Listen to this biblical prayer, which shows the heart of an "employee" who understands the heart of his "boss" as well as the heart of God: "LORD, God of my master Abraham, make me successful today, and show kindness to my master Abraham" (Genesis 24:12). Isn't that how you'd like those you lead to understand both their relationship with you and their relationship with God?

Great spiritual leaders don't rely on fear and intimidation to get people to do what needs to be done. Instead, they are kind and considerate, a kindness that grows out of strength and confidence, not from being weak-willed. And for others, undeserved kindness is a reminder of God's lasting love and infinite forgiveness.

Spirit-Filled Kindness

For a Christian, the power to respond in kindness comes from the inner working of the Holy Spirit in their lives—His work of compassion that expresses itself in outward deeds. God showers us with random acts of kindness to illustrate His love. And again, kindness is more than being nice; it's discerning another's point of pain and, with Spirit-led sensitivity, bringing them relief. A kind action can come in many forms: a gentle word, a gift, a word of wisdom, a verbal prayer, an introduction, or an affirmation.

Let kindness become a way of life and a way of leading others. Have you been wronged? If so, consider an act of kindness in response. Extend gentleness in the face of harshness. Let others know you care and are thinking of them. Give affirmation to someone weighed down by disappointment and hopelessness. Be generous to those who serve you in restaurants—ask them how they're doing and leave a nice tip. Validate your friends' feelings without prescribing solutions.

Open your home to those who need a safe and secure environment for a period of time. Let those around you know they are loved and accepted. Be patient with emotional meltdowns. Really listen not just to others' words but to the emotions their words reveal. Forgive mistakes. Try to imagine the best motives of others. Step in and help out those who are struggling with assignments that make them feel overwhelmed. Remind others of God's love and His kindness.

Kindness heals and kindness brings hope. And kindness leads to greater success.

Spiritually Mature Leaders...

- respond in kindness rather than responding in kind,

- recognize that everyone is fighting their own difficult battles,

- are proactive with kindness, not passive,

- find practical ways to show their care and compassion, and

- understand that their kindness is a reflection of God's kindness toward them.

CHAPTER 12

GOODNESS HELPS OTHERS BECOME THEIR BEST

*I myself am convinced, my brothers and sisters, that you
yourselves are full of goodness, filled with knowledge
and competent to instruct one another.*

ROMANS 15:14

*It is a grand mistake to think of being great without goodness
and I pronounce it as certain that there was never a truly
great man that was not at the same time truly virtuous.*

BENJAMIN FRANKLIN

Goodness flows out of the heart of God. Good is to God what bad is to evil. It's an expression of moral excellence and purity that streams forth from the life of any man or woman surrendered to the Holy Spirit's control. Good can be seen in the virtues that bubble up from a deep-seated belief that no real, good thing is outside of Christ. God's goodness reveals His glory to the world, the ultimate evidence that He is at work among His children.

We might say someone is a good man or a good woman, but this fails to do justice to the depth involved in their truly participating in God's goodness. Some might say a good person is someone who works hard to respond to life's challenges in a positive way, but that puts too much emphasis on the human element of goodness. At its root, goodness as a fruit of the Spirit is a supernatural quality. When we are saved, God's goodness floods our souls like a warm bath cleanses a dirty body. Our soiled soul is washed clean, and God's goodness takes permanent residence in our lives.

Goodness is a quality of the heart, and having a good heart means you have a heart governed by God. Goodness isn't about following a set of rules or principles. It's about following Jesus. Following Him recognizes that He is the moral authority over what is defined as good. We might feel good about someone, but if their morals and ethics violate Christ's code of conduct, then theirs is not a good life to emulate. Goodness isn't based on how we feel but on what God says is good.

Henri Nouwen emphasizes that goodness is seen in how we respond to the situations and people in our lives:

> I can choose to be grateful when I am criticized, even when my heart still responds in bitterness. I can choose to speak about goodness and beauty, even when my inner eye still looks for someone to accuse or something to call ugly.[9]

The kind of goodness that reflects God is both humble and bold. As followers of Christ we have a moral obligation to obey Him even when it goes against the grain of our culture. Doing the right thing is more than being a "do-gooder." It's the sign of someone committed to Jesus, whose goodness gives them the influence to change the world on His behalf.

God is calling you and me to be change agents for His glory. And we show ourselves "worthy of His calling" when we follow the path of goodness. To that end, Paul told the Thessalonians this: "We constantly pray for you, that our God may make you worthy of his calling, and that by his power he may bring to fruition your every desire for goodness and your every deed prompted by faith" (2 Thessalonians 1:11). Effective spiritual leaders have a good heart, which consists of more than following a set of principles. It recognizes the Lord is the moral authority over what is defined as good.

> Effective spiritual leaders have a good heart,
> which consists of more than following a set of
> principles. It recognizes the Lord is the moral
> authority over what is defined as good.

Do Your Best, Trust God for the Rest

God expects your best—nothing more, nothing less. He will give you the needed strength and confidence, but it's up to you to follow in obedience. Your best plus God's best is a productive combination. Be careful not to fall into the false belief that God will take care of everything without your having to expend any effort. On the other hand, don't make the mistake of believing it's all on your shoulders. God wants to come alongside and partner with you. He wants to give you the dignity of being part of accomplishing His will.

God asks you to do your best, but He also understands you have limitations. Your stage of life, giftedness, experience, availability, and wisdom all determine your capacity. The capacities of others will sometimes be greater than yours, but don't make theirs your standard. Instead, be a good steward of the responsibilities God has given to *you*. Do them well. Give everything you do your best effort, but remember you won't always accomplish all you'd like or achieve the perfection you'd like. And learn to say no when you realize requirements exceed your capacity.

Goodness in action is all about balance. An attitude of superiority can lead to pride, but discouragement is the result when you feel you have failed, fallen short of your goals. Self-flagellation will never gain you points with God or with others. Rather than respect, you'll get only pity. But if you become too "puffed up" over your achievements, just remember there's always someone who can probably do what you've done a little better.

And not everything is about numbers. Sometimes less accomplishes more if it's "a less" pointing in the right direction. Why settle for the wilderness of simple addition when you can celebrate the promised land of complex multiplication? The more you exercise your best, the better you become. Your best may even become *the* best. Reaching your potential starts with pursuing your best, with chasing after what is truly good.

Show your goodness in working hard and then rest in the fact that you've done your best for God. Do your best, trust God with the rest, and then rest in Him.

Goodness Thinks the Best of Others

One of the secrets of effective leadership is to think the best of others. When you do, they tend to think the best of you. A wonderful relational reciprocity occurs when we give others the benefit of the doubt, and they, in turn, offer us the same. If both parties have the best interests of the other in mind, a greater good can be achieved. We're always tempted to default to cynicism and suspicion, but we should push these aside and trust the results to God.

We can't judge the heart of any man or woman. Only God can. So when we pursue our responsibilities as a leader with a positive attitude toward others, we're so much more likely to get a positive result. Then we can enjoy the freedom that comes when we turn it all over to God.

One of the secrets of effective leadership
is to think the best of others. When you
do, they tend to think the best of you.

When others challenge us with tough questions, we shouldn't assume they're being critical. Instead, we should look for more clarity, connection, and accountability because of what they're asking. If we're not willing to do this, our pride will stifle an opportunity for improvement and growth. Pride so easily and so often gets in the way of making real progress. We'd rather strike out on our own without listening to what could be wise insight.

We should think the best of others because God does. When He looks at His children, He sees Christ, not just self-absorbed sinners.

He sees our potential—not just who we are at present but who we can be. Do you look at your employees and coworkers with a belief in their continuing growth, as God sees them? Or do you have them locked into a limited and negative perception?

Everyone is rough around the edges and not yet all they can be, but can we learn to accept and appreciate that? Or will we continue to have unreasonable expectations of others? Will we keep a positive and hopeful attitude, or will we give up all too quickly? Can we do what Paul encouraged in Philippians 2:3-4? "Do nothing out of selfish ambition or vain conceit. Rather, in humility value others above yourselves, not looking to your own interests but each of you to the interests of others."

The good person, filled with God's goodness, looks for goodness in others, continuing to believe in their potential even in the face of their errors and mistakes. Seeing others with goodness means seeing them through God's eyes.

A Good Daughter of Love

I've been blessed to see goodness in action.

When people lose someone they deeply love, a deep sorrow reflects that love. That's true for Rita, my beautiful wife whose mom, Jean, recently graduated to be with Jesus. My heart has ached for her, and so I wrote this note to my bride to honor the love she showed for her mom.

Dear Rita:

Your otherworldly love of laying down your life for your mother every day all these years, after she suffered a stroke, inspires and instructs me to love well. Calling her on the phone almost daily struggling to understand her expressions. Oh, how she anticipated that call every day knowing her daughter was going to love her well!! Hundreds of hours managing her healthcare, her medicine, talking to doctors and nurses. It's overwhelming to me, but the love of Jesus in you left me in awe and worship of our Savior.

It almost looks effortless because that's what love does when it's a divine expression of the heart. You loved her so well. Your patient listening. Your peaceful comfort of your dad. After the doctor visits taking her to Nicky's for a meat and three. Getting her hair done and shopping at T.J. Maxx. You were her best medicine!!

You model for me and our four daughters, four sons-in-law, and our eleven grandchildren how to love beautifully and sacrificially.

My tears mingle with yours as your mom is having all of hers wiped away.

You asked me what we will do without her. I don't know. But I know the love of Jesus that flowed through your mama's life we will never forget. And we will emulate and we will celebrate! Her legacy will outlive her for many generations through the shadow of her influence over her grandchildren and their children's children.

Your mama won her battles on her knees seeking to please an audience of one. She sat in the presence of Love to be loved, so she could love so well—as you model so well as her daughter.

I love you, sweet Rita. Love will get us through because that's what we do. That's what your mama did.

Love in Christ,
Boyd

Spiritually Mature Leaders...

- know goodness comes from the heart of God,

- don't just follow principles and rule but seek the best of God's will,

- understand that we must each do our best and then leave the rest to God,

- think the best of others in the hope they'll think the best of them, and

- try to see others through God's eyes, finding potential in everyone.

CHAPTER 13

FAITHFULNESS FINISHES WELL

Now the time is fast approaching for my release from this life and I am ready to be offered as a sacrifice. I have fought an excellent fight. I have finished my full course and I've kept my heart full of faith. There is a crown of righteousness waiting in heaven for me, and I know that my Lord will reward me on his day of righteous judgment.

2 TIMOTHY 4:6-8 TPT

You need God's direction before you can prosper in anything you do. However, it takes your choices to begin; it takes your passion to stay on; it also takes your integrity to finish it well!

ISRAELMORE AYIVOR

When we read the life stories of famous leaders in the Bible, we discover that many of them didn't finish well. They often got off to a good start, leading the people with obedience and a faithfulness to God's call. But then, for different reasons, they went off track. The same thing happens with parenting, marriages, and business endeavors. People start strong but finish poorly.

Of course, none of us want that to be true of our leadership. So how do we avoid going off the rails and crashing? I think it all comes down to the choices we make. The choices we make today will determine how we finish tomorrow. Even in the most difficult of circumstances, we can make the right choices, and perhaps that's when it's most important to make them. But we must make them even when things are going well. Otherwise, we may not only take that blessing for granted but stop seeking after the wisdom we'll need when life takes a difficult turn.

If you're like me, at the end of any endeavor, and especially at the end of my life, I don't want any regrets about the path I took to get there. That's where faithfulness comes in. We each must ask ourselves, *Am I being faithful to God, faithful to my values, faithful to the people I work with, and faithful to the vision God has given me?*

We each must ask ourselves, *Am I being faithful to God, faithful to my values, faithful to the people I work with, and faithful to the vision God has given me?*

God isn't looking for perfection, which is a good thing since none of us would be able to operate under that standard. But He desires that we be passionate about our relationship with Him and obedient to His Word. That's where faithfulness starts. The leaders who don't finish well are often those who depend on themselves rather than on God. They think they have a better plan, and they're willing to make the compromises necessary to do things their own way. The end result is often tragic—or at least disappointing.

It helps if we think about life as a marathon—not just a 50-yard dash dependent on today's decisions but an endurance test made up of our accumulated decisions over the long haul. And Jesus awaits us at the finish line. Hebrews 12:1-3 tells us He's joined there by a "great cloud of witnesses" who surround and encourage us as we run our own race. The Savior and the saints are praying for us and encouraging us to finish well.

How encouraging it is to remember that we do not run the marathon of life on our own. At every step God is with us, and as noted in the mid-twentieth-century folk song based on an old spiritual, we need to keep our "eyes on the prize" as we travel each and every mile of life's journey. If we're to finish well, we dare not stray from the path marked out for us, thinking we can find a better one. We need to be faithful and stay focused on the final destination. That focus will make a difference as we travel. We will be more faithful.

Along the way, we will surely experience the temptation to take a detour that promises a quicker and more painless way to travel. We may become worn out and ready to drop out of the race. We may have moments when we want to turn back. But when every muscle is screaming and we're breathing hard, that's exactly when we need to stay the course. And when we have the opportunity to pause for a cool drink of water and take a moment for rest and rejuvenation, we can and should take it—as long as we start again after we've rested.

Then later, after we've struggled up the hill of hope, we'll have an opportunity to enjoy the righteous run down the other side. But at every turn, we need to refer to the life map God has provided—His Word.

The marathon of life will always be easier when we're aware that God is running alongside us. We can be confident that we are never alone, and when we're near to Him, it's easier to hear Him whisper His instructions for the next leg of the race. Ultimately, spiritual leaders who finish well are those who stay focused on the ultimate prize—Christ's commendation—His "Well done, good and faithful servant." And if we think of each mile as potentially our last, we'll find it easier to remain faithful with every step.

Not only is God running alongside us but we have brothers and sisters in the same race. We need to receive and give encouragement, offer wisdom, and share some running tips with them.

Plan to Finish Well

Finishing well doesn't happen without good planning, and certainly not without counting the cost. In one of His discussions with a large crowd, Jesus used a building illustration to point out the danger in following Him without first knowing what discipleship would cost.

Suppose one of you wants to build a tower. Will you first sit down and estimate the cost to see if you have enough money to complete it? For if you lay the foundation and are not able to finish it, everyone who sees it will ridicule you, saying, "This person began to build and wasn't able to finish" (Luke 14:28-30).

We can also apply this caution to any tendency to move forward without a plan. Sure, God can bless a mess, but He normally prefers blessing a plan! When we pray and plan and prepare, we are honoring God's usual process for success. One of my friends, Mike, is a great example of this. He's highly intentional in his approach to anything he undertakes. He writes down his Spirit-led goals, and then every day he reviews them and prays over them. I'm sure he counts the cost as well.

Some of his larger goals are even printed out, laminated, and hung in a prominent place in his home and office as a reminder. He's even been known to study these goals in the shower. Now, that's a bit over-the-top for me, but it works for him. He's been highly successful in every area of his life. And he's a great leader.

Planning well involves counting the cost of commitment and understanding your dedication to Christ is priority one on your to-do list. The one who's submitted to the authority of Christ is a disciple, and a faithful disciple chooses well today and finishes well tomorrow. Finishing well does not imply a perfect life, but it does require a life submitted to God.

> Finishing well does not imply a perfect life,
> but it does require a life submitted to God.

You'll need fuel along the way if you want to finish well, and studying and applying God's Word will give you the daily strength you need for daily choices. His Word will inspire, inform, and invigorate your marathon of life. Then as you discern God's best every day, you can follow Him wholeheartedly. In addition, the faithfulness you achieve will earn you the credibility required when you need people to trust your leadership.

Not only are God and the saints watching you, but family members, board members, employees, and other leaders are watching as well. That means you might unexpectantly be a role model for someone. So pace yourself by God's grace, stay faithful and true, remain on course, and keep pointing people to the strength you find in your faith. The race of righteousness will sweat out some of your sinful thinking and renew your mind. Unrighteous anger will be replaced by patience, fear by trust, pride by humility, and addictions by freedom. As you run the race, you'll grow stronger and more fit with every mile.

Always remember that you are in the middle of the race. If you've made major mistakes or strayed off course, it's never too late to get back on track. God loves to work through your false starts and backsliding and put you back on the road to finishing well. If it's time to restart your run, just call on the One who wants to lead you every step of the way.

Faithful Daily Until We See Jesus Face-to-Face

Faithfulness is doing what you said you would do. It's an integrity issue, and commitments are not to be taken lightly.

A verbal commitment is still a contract. However, they can be the most risky and easily misunderstood. If we make a verbal commitment, it behooves us to make sure it's plainly understood by all parties involved. Without a clear understanding, there can be miscommunication and a perception of unfaithfulness. The burden of responsibility is on the communicator. If we're moving fast and overcommitted, our communication skills and follow-through suffer. We may assume others understand us and know what's going on, but this is a dicey assumption. So slow down and communicate more. (Also show up for appointments on time.)

Less is more. Most of us would be much better off if we focused on fewer commitments. Take a relational audit and ask others if they perceive you as being faithful to your commitments to them. Don't blame others for unfaithfulness if that's a chronic problem in your own life. Fortunately, as followers of Christ, we have Him as our faithful model.

The Lord is faithful to the faithful, but He is also faithful even in our unfaithfulness. God says what He will do and does what He says. He is faithful to forgive our sin and lead us to forgive others. He is faithful to convict us of sin and lead us into righteousness. He is faithful to flood our souls with peace, joy, and contentment. God understands what it means to keep a commitment, even at great cost. After all, He allowed the death of His only Son to save us.

Unfaithfulness, however, will catch up with us if it's not quickly remedied. Adultery is an example of marital unfaithfulness, yet how many of us go to bed with other conflicting relational commitments. We must not let work, hobbies, children, or money become our "mistress." Faithfulness begins and ends with follow-through on our commitments to God.

After our conversion, we made a commitment to follow Christ. Following Him requires fidelity of faith. There can be no equals to our love for Him. In His Word He says to let our yes be yes and our no be no, so we must follow through. We want to be faithful to Him and others.

Your faithfulness does not go unnoticed or unrewarded. One of the greatest rewards is the gift of trust. Faithfulness births and grows trust, so over time you earn the reputation of being a trustworthy person. Those who can be trusted with a little can be trusted with much. Thus, be faithful so you can be trusted. In Jesus's parable of the bags of gold, the master said, "Well done, good and faithful servant! You have been faithful with a few things; I will put you in charge of many things. Come and share your master's happiness!"

Above all, be faithful because God is faithful!

Spiritually Mature Leaders...

- understand that their everyday choices are the key to finishing well,

- know that God is looking for passion more than perfection,

- realize that others are always paying attention to their actions,

- seek to be faithful every day in every way, and

- stay focused on the ultimate reward of faithfulness—pleasing God.

CHAPTER 14

GENTLENESS COMFORTS HURTING HEARTS

Your God says to you: Comfort, comfort my people with gentle, compassionate words. Speak tenderly from the heart.

ISAIAH 40:1-2 TPT

I'm here. I love you. I don't care if you need to stay up crying all night long, I will stay with you. If you need the medication again, go ahead and take it—I will love you through that, as well. If you don't need the medication, I will love you, too. There's nothing you can ever do to lose my love. I will protect you until you die, and after your death I will still protect you. I am stronger than Depression and I am braver than Loneliness and nothing will ever exhaust me.

ELIZABETH GILBERT, *EAT, PRAY, LOVE*[10]

A wise old saying goes like this: you can catch more flies with honey than with vinegar. Now, I'm not certain that catching flies is at the top of my to-do list, but this little phrase is worth keeping in mind for every leader. What it emphasizes is that a gentle approach is most often the best way to achieve the goals we're trying to reach.

Often gentleness isn't our first instinct when we're dealing with a problem person. But if we learn to approach everyone with gentleness and kindness, we'll have an easier time solving the difficulties that can come up whenever we're dealing with other human beings—whether peers or any people we lead.

Our model for gentleness is our Lord Himself. Although Jesus could be aggressive and confrontational when necessary—and sometimes confrontation *is* necessary—most often He was humble, gentle, and comforting. He said, "Take my yoke upon you and learn from me, for I am gentle and humble in heart, and you will find rest for your souls" (Matthew 11:29). His first approach was kindness. Gentleness does not negate the aggressiveness that's occasionally necessary, nor does a spirit of humility eliminate courage. Jesus is the king of all creation and ruler over the world, but He rules and leads with gentleness and humility. That is the paradox at the heart of who He is.

Like Jesus, good leaders know they must use their power carefully. Gentle and humble leaders use their position to serve others and help them be their best. They know a team is strengthened more effectively by encouragement and affirmation than by humiliation and criticism. To one degree or another, everyone has a fragile ego, and the leaders who respect that reality are better prepared to navigate their relationships, both personal and professional.

A gentle and humble approach increases the probability of success because it lets people know you care about them and their feelings, not just the positive outcome of a project they're working on. If people cower at your power, it might feed your ego, but it destroys theirs. There's no need to inflict fear as a mode of operation. Honestly, promoting fear is the leadership technique of the insecure and incompetent leader.

Promoting fear is the leadership technique
of the insecure and incompetent leader.

Just because intimidation might work in the short term is no excuse for using it. Of course, sometimes you might need to call someone on the carpet for sloppiness, inattention, or disloyalty. But even then the best leaders know this is an opportunity to provide stability and calm rather than to raise the level of intensity. Keeping a gentle and caring demeanor shows, at root, a trust in the Lord and a dependence on His leading. And gentleness is a great lubricant for every relationship. It keeps things running with much less friction.

It's probably inevitable that some people will try to take advantage of you when you use the gentle approach, but over the long haul, humility wins. With humility, you win over people. You win over accounts. You win over problems with less stress and drama. You win over adversity, and you build deeper loyalty. You win respect from others for your evenhandedness as you operate toward them with respect. Anyone who feels respected is more committed to the team—and to you. Most important of all, you win the blessing of God. A leader can never go wrong following the character qualities of Jesus.

So remember that your position of influence as a parent, pastor, spouse, executive, volunteer, sole proprietor, or teacher should never be a place to stroke your own ego through aggression...or even passive aggression. Instead, use your influence to gently lead by example. And when it's necessary to confront others, do it with gentleness and understanding rather than tear them down with criticism. And don't get stuck on your own agenda. Listen and learn. That'll make you a much better leader.

To stay gentle is to walk in one of the fruits of the Spirit. Putting our pride aside is the result of daily seeking the filling and leading of the Holy Spirit as well as being open to finding God's wisdom in every situation we face (Ephesians 3:14-19). One who is broken before God and more aligned with His purposes will find that gentleness has been grafted onto their soul.

You can be bold and forthright if that's your natural personality. Gentleness doesn't have to be milquetoast. But whatever your personality type, do everything from a heart that's gentle and humble. Deflect attention away from yourself, and trust God that you'll get your recognition in due time. Heap praise on those who need to hear your words of encouragement rather than respond in arrogance and pride. Gentleness, humility, and comfort are the triplets birthed from being transformed by Jesus.

Gentleness Offers Comfort

Even your best followers may need an extra dose of comfort from time to time. We live and work with broken people in a broken world, and we all have our own areas of brokenness. If you've ever pounded on an appliance that wasn't functioning well, you quickly learned it didn't help. In fact, your pounding made the problem worse. You needed to find out what caused the malfunction and go from there.

Working with people is the same. Start by taking the time to learn what's making them malfunction, approaching them with a gentle spirit.

I remember how broken I felt as I attended the memorial service for my beloved mother. It was the saddest day of my life; I knew it was unlikely that anyone would ever love me quite like she did. There would be no human substitute for her single-minded love for her sons. As a single parent, she knew she had to carry an expanded capacity for love to fill the void in our lives with no father in our home. She did so selflessly. As I wept and mourned over my mother, my tears were a tribute to her love and the way she raised me.

But as I wept, I didn't weep alone. Friends and family offered comfort and sympathy and hugs. They cried along with me. That shared grief and sorrow were an important part of my healing and moving on after such a huge loss. Then I allowed that experience to raise my own level of sympathy toward and empathy for others, and I've continued to use it as a reservoir to draw from when others need my care and attention.

Quiet, grieving tears invite the compassionate love and comfort of gentle Jesus, so don't waste your sorrows.

Quiet, grieving tears invite the compassionate love and comfort of gentle Jesus, so don't waste your sorrows.

In the Beatitudes, Jesus said, "Blessed are those who mourn, for they will be comforted" (Matthew 5:4). Sorrow, whether little or much, is an everyday occurrence on planet Earth, and we can best process our own grief by grieving along with others and helping them heal. If we ignore their grief, whether through self-absorption or embarrassment, we miss an opportunity to be healed ourselves. And we miss an opportunity to learn how to comfort.

Second Corinthians 1:3-4 says, "Praise be to the God and Father of our Lord Jesus Christ, the Father of compassion and the God of all comfort, who comforts us in all our troubles, so that we can comfort those in any trouble with the comfort we ourselves receive from God."

What sorrows lie deep on the bottom of your soul? What sorrows have you suppressed that cry out for comfort and grieving? Maybe abuse has robbed you of your dignity, or the wound of a severed relationship still festers in anger and bitterness. Perhaps you've never fully acknowledged your own sorrow. Or maybe you never really mourned a life-altering experience by receiving the healing love and comfort of others. Sometimes it's hard to be honest about our own woundedness. Like learning a new language, you might stumble over the words to express your emotions. Perhaps letting your tears do the talking is best at times.

When you learn to cry out to Christ and to others, you'll find compassion and comfort. And when you embrace these gifts, you'll be equipped with the key element needed for gentleness.

The Power of Words

We all know the power of words to transform any situation, and gentle words can have a particularly transformative effect. In the book of Proverbs, Solomon points to gentleness as an antidote that gives life rather than death: "A gentle tongue is a tree of life, but perverseness in it breaks the spirit" (Proverbs 15:4 ESV). Calm conversations contribute to healing and avoid hurt. They offer words that build up a person's spirit rather than breaking it. Kind and tender speech offers hope, understanding, and acceptance. It can sound something like, "How can I help you accomplish what needs to get done today?" Gentleness can also offer gratitude: "Thanks for helping me think through this issue. I need your wisdom and perspective." Gentleness expresses itself with humble honesty as well: "I'm worried about the future and could use your prayers."

Gentleness is another word for graciousness. We grow gentler as we grow in grace. Grace is the engine that powers a gentle heart, and gracious words are the fruit of a life rooted in God. An old Shaker hymn from 1867, "Gentle Words," was written as our country was still healing from the Civil War:

> What the dew is to the flower,
> Gentle words are to the soul.
> And a blessing to the giver,
> And so dear to the receiver.
> We should never withhold.
> Gentle words, kindly spoken,
> Often soothe the troubled mind.
> While links of love are broken
> By words that are unkind.
> Then O, thou gentle spirit,
> My constant Guardian be.
> "Do to others" be my motto,
> "As I have them do to me."

This hymn is such a perfect expression of the power of gentle words from a gentle heart, and we should apply words of comfort and truth as a tourniquet for those who suffer cuts inflicted by betrayal, lies, or abuse.

We should apply words of comfort and truth as a tourniquet for those who suffer cuts inflicted by betrayal, lies, or abuse.

I've found that when I'm exhausted or feeling overwhelmed, I'm more susceptible to a sinful approach with my tongue. If something doesn't go my way, I can become grumpy or demanding with my words. So I've learned to be especially aware of what I say when I'm not at my best. It's all too easy to take out my fears and frustrations on others with harsh phrases like "You really don't care or understand," "You never think or plan ahead," or "You always [fill in the blank]!" Such phrases only aggravate a situation and agitate the people involved.

The better response is to pause, be quiet, pray, and then speak from a Spirit-led gentleness. Learn and use a vocabulary of care and phrases that encourage, comfort, and heal.

We are governed by gentleness when the cadence of our conversation isn't high-pitched with rapid-fire reactions. So take the time to *respond* rather than just *react*. When you use respectful dialogue without angrily attacking the motives of others, you can bring God's grace to the table rather than a "know it all" attitude. Our attitude makes a difference. As Peter wrote in reference to our testimony, "Always be prepared to give an answer to everyone who asks you to give the reason for the hope that you have. But do this with gentleness and respect" (1 Peter 3:15). Your motive for extending comfort is your own gratitude to God for His comfort in your life.

Your motive for extending comfort is your own
gratitude to God for His comfort in your life.

As a leader, you have the opportunity to be a facilitator of God's comfort. Yet you are not responsible for the recipient's immediate reaction. Lingering anger or bitterness may blunt their ability to feel or express gratitude. Deep hurt may hinder their weak prayers. But as God has comforted you, so have you been given the opportunity to comfort others. Watch your attitude. Don't overreact. Season your speech with gentleness. You'll find that you can be a blessing to others as well as lead them toward becoming loyal members of the team you lead.

Spiritually Mature Leaders...

- refuse to use fear and intimidation to get people to do what they want them to do,

- listen carefully and compassionately to the hurt in other people's hearts,

- apply words of comfort as a tourniquet for those who suffer cuts inflicted by betrayal, lies, or abuse,

- lean on God for comfort so they have a reservoir of compassion for others, and

- know the power of pausing, quieting their soul, and praying so they can speak from a place of Spirit-led gentleness.

CHAPTER 15

SELF-CONTROL CHANNELS PASSION APPROPRIATELY

Do nothing out of selfish ambition or vain conceit.
Rather, in humility value others above yourselves, not
looking to your own interests but each of you to the
interests of the others. In your relationships with one
another, have the same mindset as Christ Jesus.

PHILIPPIANS 2:3-5

No conflict is so severe as his who labors to subdue himself.

THOMAS À KEMPIS

Rita and I celebrated our fortieth wedding anniversary with a trip to Greece, and the highlight was the day we toured the ruins of Olympia, the home of the first Olympic Games. They took place more than 700 years before Jesus's time on earth.

From our guide, Studi, we learned about some strict expectations for the participants. Every four years, those invited to compete were required to arrive 30 days before the first event, so the judges could observe their interaction with fellow athletes. They were especially looking for the qualities of humility, honesty, and deference to peers. Each of those qualities demands first mastering the virtue of self-control, and as role models, how the athletes behaved was important.

The apostle Paul often used the language of competitive sports as a metaphor for living out the Christian life. This leader among leaders knew becoming the right kind of person isn't an easy matter; it doesn't just happen magically but requires focus, conviction, and hard work.

He wrote this in his first letter to the Corinthians:

> Athletes in training are very strict with themselves, exercising self-control over desires, and for what? For a wreath that soon withers or is crushed or simply forgotten. That is not our race. We run for the crown that we will wear for eternity. So I don't run aimlessly. I don't let my eyes drift from the finish line (1 Corinthians 9:25-26 THE VOICE).

Like an athlete, Paul is saying, we need to keep our purpose in mind and never lose focus on the goals that really matter—the heavenly rewards, not the temporal earthly prizes. We need self-control. Not allowing ourselves to be buffeted about by our changing desires or giving in to our worst instincts but learning to control ourselves—the way we act, the way we talk, and the attitudes we display.

Paul was himself a practical illustration of what self-control looks like in action. He didn't take advantage of others, and he especially didn't take advantage of his position as an apostle. He quietly and selflessly worked his day job as a tentmaker so he wouldn't be a burden on others. With his education and experience, he could have strutted about his accomplishments and called on others to do his bidding. But instead, he submitted his will to Jesus. He stayed loyal to his calling even when it became dangerous and controversial. He kept his eyes on the prize. He kept his eyes on Jesus.

How focused and self-controlled is your life? Are you working toward a destination? Or are you all over the map? Have you allowed the Holy Spirit to map out your life?

The self-controlled leader has a plan. And when you have a plan and have things under control, you've created margin to help others and make a difference in their lives. Watch out for the kind of busyness that keeps you hopping but isn't going anywhere meaningful. Learn to be more intentional with your time. Carefully and prayerfully work on your agenda. You'll waste less time, you'll get more done, and you'll be able to serve others through your work.

Would you qualify for God's spiritual Olympics? Do you have the kind of self-controlled character He's looking for? When people see you coming, are they energized by the opportunity to work with you? Or do they want to run and hide because they fear you'll deplete them through your self-absorption?

Learning self-control often starts with little things—excesses that get us into the most trouble. Maybe you need to change some habits. Try using a smaller plate at dinner so you eat more modestly, then skip dessert. Decide to say no to a disproportionate number of pleasures, such as yet another latest-model driver for your golf game. Be content with the car you already own instead of purchasing a new one. Stay off the internet when you might be tempted to surf sites that aren't good for you to be on. Limit the number of hours you work or the days you travel so you're home with your family more often.

With the strength of the Spirit, these small choices can lead to a better way of living and working. They build the kind of self-control that makes you a better leader. Why? Because they teach you to stay focused on God's big picture rather than on your own whims of the moment.

Exposure to the Enemy

Lack of self-control puts us squarely in the crosshairs of the enemy of our souls. When our defenses are compromised, we lose the ability to manage our emotions and think rationally. As a mayor governs a city, so must we govern our own lives. Until we do, we have no real business trying to help other people govern theirs. Until we do, we'll continue to make poor decisions, choosing anger over understanding, lust over love, greed over generosity, and our personal agenda over the bigger team agenda.

Lack of self-control puts us squarely in the crosshairs of the enemy of our souls.

Biblical boundaries are essential if we're to keep our minds and hearts and lives under control. You wouldn't walk your dog down the median of a busy highway, where any sudden lunge from him could spell disaster and death. So you shouldn't put yourself in situations that might tempt you beyond your ability to refrain. It isn't wise to linger in compromising situations. To do so could put your reputation at risk. Learn to say no, and you'll retain both your reputation with people and your purity before God.

We shouldn't think of self-control only as a defensive weapon against the Enemy. It can actually be an offensive weapon, promoting strong character and a clear conscience. It stands tall whether the culture hisses or applauds. It isn't looking for approval. Self-control is not the product of mediocrity but a strong stand for high moral values. Effective spiritual leaders use self-control to grow character with a clear conscience.

But how can we lead others if we can't lead ourselves? That's why self-control is listed as a fruit of the Spirit, and perhaps it's placed last in Paul's list because every other quality in some way rises as we exercise self-control.

Effective spiritual leaders use self-control to
grow character with a clear conscience.

Spirit-Led Choices

At its root, self-control comes in staying reliant on the Holy Spirit. It uses the gasoline of grace to govern the engine of a disciple's activity. Self-control is Spirit-control. It bows to no ego, surrendering only to Christ.

A freedom comes when we're not tossed hither and yon by our momentary whims and desires. We have the freedom to make good choices rather than be determined by our desires and emotions and insecurities. We have the freedom to say no to our body's wishes. Wise leaders know their bodies are effective servants but not good masters When Christ controls us, we become capable of controlling our lives. That, my friends, is the truest form of freedom.

The freedom of self-control can help us break *unholy* habits and replace them with *holy* habits. This isn't just the discipline of saying no; it's the mindset that comes from being mastered by Christ's preferences. There's no room for self-reliance in the Spirit-controlled life. And we can't wait to practice it until it's convenient. Now is the time to begin.

The freedom of self-control can help us break *unholy* habits and replace them with *holy* habits.

Initiate self-control in your sexual thoughts and desires, and place boundaries around what you read and watch. Pay attention to your conversations to guard them against being coarse or cynical or hurtful. Learn to remain silent rather than spew unkindness. Eat smaller portions and more healthy food. Get enough sleep by going to bed earlier. Turn off your computer in the evening and set your phone aside. Focus on the people in your life. Organize your calendar and get control of your schedule. Create a budget and stick to it. Honor the Sabbath principle of rest.

If that all sounds like hard work, here's the deal: it might be difficult at first, but in the end, the results will feel like freedom and liberation.

Passion Under Control

There's nothing wrong with passion. Passion gives us focus and gets things done. When we're looking for good employees, passion is a quality we naturally seek out. We admire people with passion. Passion brings energy into the room and sparks creativity.

But not all passion is healthy passion. We need to be passionate about the right things and not become intemperately passionate about things that don't matter or are actually unhealthy for us. What we need is a foundational passion for Christ, and then all our other passions can find their proper place.

So ask yourself, *Am I enslaved by selfish passions and pleasures? Or do I enjoy passionate living for the Lord?* For example, an all-consuming passion to make as much money as possible looks much different than a disciplined routine that passionately focuses on caring for your physical and spiritual health while investing in family and friends. If you're always emotionally spent from a frantic pace of life, you have nothing left to give when you spend time with those you love most. And you'll never be able to focus on the needs of those who follow you.

Ask the Spirit to help you take an inventory of your activities and see where some pruning might be needed. You can even overdo good activities! As a leader, you need to have a high standard of self-control over self-indulgence. Let your life be an example of passion well placed and the freedom of self-control.

Spiritually Mature Leaders...

- understand and embrace the power of self-control,

- are aware that lack of self-control is one of the weapons our Enemy can use,

- know that true freedom includes freedom from being controlled by their desires,

- model the quality of self-control for everyone on their team, and

- replace self-reliance and self-indulgence with Spirit-reliance and self-control.

Ken Boa is the president of Reflections Ministries, an organization focusing on spiritual formation, and the author of more than a dozen books on spiritual growth and spiritual disciplines. We sat down to talk about leadership in the context of the spiritual life, and here are a few of the most insightful thoughts he shared:

> Even if a person has a rich encounter with Scripture and prayer and meditation, or whatever disciplines are involved, what does that person do the rest of the day? That has rarely been taken seriously except for a nod here and there to Brother Lawrence. But really, the metaphors and the images in Scripture imply an ongoing practice of that presence.

> Most people today, especially men, have flabby wills, sloppy thought lives, and anemic aspirations. Flabby wills—that is to say they are soft; they haven't been trained; it's not pretty to see. Then sloppy thought lives, because they allow the entry of thoughts that are unworthy of their identity as followers of Jesus. And then the third one is anemic intentions, aspirations, and passions. I believe that a person is shaped by what they seek, what they long for. We become more and more conformed by that to which we aspire, and so a holy aspiration is a huge component of this.

If people took the spiritual disciplines—for example, this training in righteousness and becoming conformed more and more into the image of Christ (there's the whole idea of being transformed by that relationship)—if we took those habits and those intentions as seriously as we do any sport or any musical instrument or any kind of component that has to do with being on the stage, learning a language, or whatever, there would be a radical transformation in the church around the world.

———

A good leader will show grace, and the realization that someone's performance may not have been entirely intentional but a composition of a number of things, possibly including pain, difficulties, or setbacks. One not only prays for them, which is a priestly act, representing God before them and them before God, but one is also listening to the quiet promptings of the Spirit of God and the Spirit who gives insight as to what to ask, what to say. You are walking by the Spirit, praying for this person; you're immersing yourself into that. You're looking at them carefully for the nonverbal cues, because there are about 400,000 nonverbal cues.

———

As C.S. Lewis put it, God's the invisible master of ceremonies who puts people together in ways you could have never construed. So you need to be open to that, because if you grasp that, "Ah, this may have been a kairos moment," what at first appeared to be an interruption may have been an invitation. So now while you might have been annoyed by this person or whatever, it becomes an invitation. Having received that invitation, and you develop this by habituation and training, this understanding, you can then discern the prompting of the Spirit of God for this person, and so deep calls unto deep.

———

We tend to manage time tightly to accomplish objectives. Jesus managed time loosely enough to enhance relationships. So consider, then, when suddenly a blind person, a beggar, a leper, someone who was demon-possessed—whatever it was—what did Jesus do every time? He drove His disciples nuts because He'd stop, and suddenly He would reduce His world to that person's world, and He knew that was the Father's invitation. I love that.

———

As you know, people don't know how to listen very well. We have courses on how to speak, we learn how to write and read, but we never learn how to listen. So we just reinforce poor habits. One of those is stepping on people's ideas—jumping to conclusions, not listening carefully, not giving them the attention, not using eye contact—because the fact is we can hear about four times faster than people can speak. That gives us a lot of time, and we can either use it to wander and think of other things, or we can immerse ourselves in the precious present, which is all we've got, by immersing ourselves in that person's world. And suddenly that world becomes everything. And so, wherever you are, be all there. That becomes my highest priority, what I am called to do at the point of action.

———

I don't want to be foolish. Humility doesn't mean that you're going to be a Caspar Milquetoast and a doormat, but rather, there are going to be boundaries that are sometimes going to be necessary, and that's where wisdom comes in. So the hard play is always going to be between those two components. On the one hand, divine sovereignty; on the other hand, human responsibility. In the one hand it is faith; in the other hand is wisdom. So we move back-and-forth.

———

There are three biblical metaphors for leadership. The leader, as I see it, is a steward, a shepherd, and a servant. A steward is someone who is managing the affairs and the resources of another. The shepherd is the one who has been given the position of oversight. And a servant sees service as his practice. So we all are called in one respect or another to be a leader in those dynamics.

———

A person will learn more about themselves in a half-day encounter [with solitude and silence] than they probably otherwise would in a whole year. But most won't do it, even if they put it in their calendar. It's the best investment there can be, because it endures. I love the idea of transmuting the currency of that which is passing away—time, talent, and treasure—into the currency that will endure forever, because the other two realms of stewardship are truth and people, and so truth is a stewardship. To whom much has been given, much will be required. When you have these regular dynamic encounters before God, it becomes more and more a part of your being, a part of your practice, your aspiration, and it will spill over in the way you treat people, the way you serve them, the way you listen to them, the way you care for them, the way you pray for them, and the way you practice His presence by sometimes just silently lifting them up to the Father in all of this.

PART THREE

THE SPIRITUAL PRACTICES OF A LEADER

CHAPTER 16

CONVERSATIONAL PRAYER

*In order to keep me from becoming conceited, I was given
a thorn in my flesh, a messenger of Satan, to torment
me. Three times I pleaded with the Lord to take it away
from me. But he said to me, "My grace is sufficient for
you, for my power is made perfect in weakness."*

2 Corinthians 12:7-9

*Prayer is the natural outgushing of a soul in communion with
Jesus. Just as the leaf and the fruit will come out of the vine-
branch without any conscious effort on the part of the branch,
but simply because of its living union with the stem, so prayer
buds, and blossoms, and fruits out of souls abiding in Jesus.*

Charles Spurgeon

Every relationship requires communication to keep it healthy. Can
you imagine if you rarely talked with your spouse or your children?
Or if you never let coworkers or the people you lead know what you're
thinking? Or if you never listen to what's on their minds? Of course,
any really meaningful relationship would be impossible without sitting
down and talking things through on a regular basis. The same holds
true for your relationship with God. Though He is the invisible partner in the conversation, He still desires to hear from you and speak to
you. Prayer is the most powerful tool He can use to accomplish that.

Prayer isn't complicated. It's simply a dialogue with God, an intimate conversation with Him, and a means of staying connected with His heart. It's also a means for getting things done, for bringing God's resources to bear on the things that concern us. But before it's a means of asking for things, it's a means for drawing closer to Him. As Mother Teresa once said, "Prayer is not asking. Prayer is putting oneself in the hands of God, at His disposition, and listening to His voice in the depth of our hearts."

Nor is prayer a monologue. It isn't just filling the air with our own thoughts and needs and desires. It should be a two-way dialogue. It's the place where we open our hearts in honesty, admitting our need, and then receive wisdom and guidance as God whispers into our hearts.

Sometimes, though, prayer doesn't need to involve words at all. Sometimes it just consists of quietly sitting in the presence of God, open and receptive to His love and leading.

Love and Communion

When we seek God, we find love. We find strength, encouragement, guidance, comfort, and peace. We receive the things we need in our human friendships at an even greater level in prayer. We receive a resource we can draw on in loving others well. God loves us, so we are compelled to love others, and we learn to look for opportunities to help rather than always looking to our own needs first. We also win the war with our fleshly desires when, by faith, we wave the white flag over always wanting our own way.

Last, we gain wisdom we need as leaders. Yes, we can often force people to do what we want them to do by the power of our position, but how much wiser is it to win them to our agenda with an example of love? Our selfishness is our biggest obstacle to sacrificial love.

We win the war with our fleshly desires
when, by faith, we wave the white flag
over always wanting our own way.

Jesus is our model for sacrificial love. He laid down His life to save the lives of others. His humble act of surrender to His heavenly Father inspires us to surrender ourselves to Him. But we can never hope to offer this kind of love under our own power. Such goodness and graciousness are not ours to give unless we've been recipients of them through our relationship with Jesus. Our communion with Christ in prayer is the school where we learn how to live in a Christlike manner.

And in that school of prayer, we learn of the tenderness of God and to let what breaks His heart break our own hearts. There, we learn to confront injustice with tough love. There, we learn to be kind and giving not only to those we love but even to strangers. There, we experience a depth of love that not only transforms us but gives us a message of transformation to share with the lost, the hurt, and the broken.

Childlike Prayer

One of the things that can keep us from praying is our tendency to make prayer more complicated than it needs to be. There's no set of secrets you need to learn, or any profound mystical state you have to attain, or a set of theological affirmations you must understand. No, prayer is, at its heart, simple. It's just a matter of having an intimate conversation with the God who loves you.

Rita has a simple prayer routine when she tucks in our grandchildren at bedtime. She places her hands near their ears and prays for them to hear the truth of God's love and not be deceived by the devil's lies. She places her fingers above their eyes and asks the Lord to protect their sight from evil and focus their vision on what is pure and pleasing to the heavenly Father. Last, she cups her hand over their chests and prays for peace to guard their hearts and minds in Christ. One night our three-year-old grandson tugged her sleeve and said, "You forgot to pray for my nose!"

Simple prayers, then, can be the most powerful. We don't need to make them complicated. We don't have to find the exact right words. Prayer isn't an exercise in eloquence. But we do need to be emotionally vulnerable and honest in our conversation with God, and childlike prayer is emotionally honest in its expression. Learning this emotional honesty not only gives power to our prayers but helps us be more emotionally honest in our other relationships, including those where we are a leader. We need to be emotionally open and let others know they can be open with us, that they can tell us what they're really feeling without being afraid they're putting themselves at risk. God is willing to listen to our rants, and sometimes we need to be open to patiently hearing the rants of those who are unhappy with us or need to unburden themselves.

> Childlike prayer is emotionally
> honest in its expression.

The mark of mature followers of Jesus is that their prayers become ever more childlike. They realize they're helplessly dependent on God, so they raise their voices in prayer and praise no matter what circumstances they find themselves in. They go to Him in raw honesty and absolute vulnerability. So ask yourself, *Are my prayers dry and predictable? Or do they have the urgency and anticipation of a child? Are they joyful over God's generosity, His goodness, and His joy? And are they true to what I'm feeling at the moment I'm expressing them?*

God meets us where we are, so we never have to hide behind our dignity or our concern over what others may think. Every leader needs to have childlike conversations with God.

Ongoing Conversation

In 1 Thessalonians 5:17, Paul tells us to "pray without ceasing" (ESV). Now, that can sound like a pretty impossible task if we don't understand what he was getting at. He didn't mean we should all join a monastery and spend 24 hours a day on our knees. What he meant, I think, is that our conversation with God is an open channel. With or without using words, we're in contact with Him all the time.

Conversational prayer is an ongoing sacred communion with the Father, Son, and Holy Spirit. When we became followers of Jesus, we were born into His spiritual ecosystem. The air of His environment is pure and cleansing, so we can learn to use our spiritual lungs to breathe in the oxygen of God, who is ever present with us. We pray without ceasing when our souls inhale the Spirit and exhale self. When we don't pray, it's like holding our breath. We don't get the spiritual oxygen we so desperately need, and we become more vulnerable to lies and deceptions. We smother our faith as we deny our souls the air of prayer.

Prayer requires an attitude of openness. In prayer, we don't have to prove our point, and we certainly shouldn't try to shift the blame for our failings to someone else. (Isn't prayer, in that way, a good model for our conversations with others?) Whenever we become aware of a need, prayer is the first place we should go. When we're confused and need wisdom, prayer is the first place we should go. When we're anxious or fearful, prayer is the first place we should go. And when we pray without ceasing, prayer becomes our reflexive response. We always go first to God.

When we pray, we discover peace and calm, a more tempered response to difficult circumstances, and a ray of hope even in the darkest times. But prayer shouldn't always be a response to trouble. More often it should be a cry of gratitude, praise, and continued commitment. If the only time you pray is when you're in trouble, your spiritual life is in trouble!

If the only time you pray is when you're in trouble, your spiritual life is in trouble!

In everything we give thanks to God with a posture of humble prayer. Even when our health fails, we thank Him for the healthy life we've enjoyed. Whether or not He heals us, we are grateful for His goodness. As we pray without ceasing, we find ourselves more alert to the Spirit's promptings to give time or resources to someone who needs them or to listen to Him and change course.

Prayer is the oxygen we need to keep moving forward along the path to which God has called us. It keeps us in touch with the One who loves us most.

Spiritually Mature Leaders...

- know prayer is a dialogue, not a monologue,

- bring the vulnerability and honesty of prayer into their conversations with others,

- embrace a childlike approach to prayer,

- learn the secret of ongoing sacred communication with God, and

- respond to the prompting they receive from the Holy Spirit.

CHAPTER 17

GOD'S WORD: SOUL FOOD

Your word is a lamp to my feet, a light on my path.

<small>Psalm 119:105</small>

Some people like to read so many [Bible] chapters every day. I would not dissuade them from the practice, but I would rather lay my soul asoak in half a dozen verses all day than rinse my hand in several chapters. Oh, to be bathed in a text of Scripture, and to let it be sucked up in your very soul, till it saturates your heart!

<small>Charles Spurgeon</small>

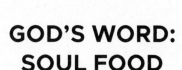here's nothing like a great meal. This morning, as I read and reflected in our library, my stomach started to rumble with hunger. Just like clockwork, the door opened, and there was my sweet wife with a small plate of soft scrambled eggs, nicely enhanced by melted goat cheese and sautéed spinach. It was like manna from heaven! The first few bites started to curb my hunger, and then I began to savor each and every bite of the tasty, satisfying, and simple feast.

Have my words made you hungry? Words can do that. Just as my body needs the nutrition and taste of a good meal, so my soul hungers for morsels of love, hope, wisdom, and grace, which have all been prepared by God. The psalmist spoke of the gourmet feast that awaited him in the Word of God: "How sweet are your words to my taste, sweeter than honey to my mouth! I gain understanding from your precepts; therefore I hate every wrong path" (Psalm 119:103-104). The honey from the Lord's hive of wisdom complements all the other intense flavors that await the palate of faith.

The whole of Psalm 119, from which that passage is taken, is a celebration of the wonder and beauty of both God's world and His Word. In a devotional commentary about this psalm, Charles Spurgeon wrote, "It is known among the Germans as 'The Christians' golden A B C of the praise, love, power, and use of the Word of God'...Each portion of the Psalm begins with a letter of the Hebrew alphabet."

He went on to call it the "golden psalm," just as many refer to it today. He also said,.

> All human books grow stale after a time; but with the Word of God the desire to study it increases, while the more you know of it the less you think you know. The Book grows upon you: as you dive into its depths you have a fuller perception of the infinity which remains unexplored. You are still sighing to enjoy more of that which it is your bliss to taste.[11]

All other currencies of worldly wisdom are cheap and stale counterfeits compared to the profound golden but practical precepts from God. They rarely if ever send you into "sighing to enjoy more of that which it is your bliss to taste." They not only bring delight but offer a path through life. They are spiritual nutrition offered by the One who knows exactly what we need. When digested, they bring strength and peace to our souls. And Jesus, the living Word, curates them for each of us.

Jesus was the Word become flesh (John 1:14), and He invites us all to experience His life. Just as the Israelites depended on manna from heaven during their long trek through the wilderness, so is Jesus our Bread of Life. His life and words will help us make our way through the struggles we face. The written Word (Scripture) and the living Word (Jesus) work together to give us wisdom for living. All of us who are leaders need this wisdom for our own lives as well as for guiding and leading others on the right path.

Dallas Willard, one of the great spiritual leaders of our time, describes the transformational power of the Bible and the need to experience it, not just believe it:

> Sometimes in churches we work to get people to affirm stuff, even though they don't believe in it like they believe in gravity. So somebody will say, "I believe that the Bible is the inspired, authoritative Word of God." But the Bible says it is more blessed to give than to receive, yet they are not giving. So, do they really believe that the Bible is the authoritative, inspired Word of God? Well, at one level, they think they do, but the most important level of belief is their mental map of reality. What are those perceptions that actually guide how we live, what we do? Because that is simply how reality looks to us. What we want to do is not simply teach doctrine and get people to affirm it. We want to help people have the same mental map that Jesus had of how things are.[12]

The point, Willard is saying, is not just to gather good teachings and memorable quotes from the Bible but to live its message and let it change the way we think and feel. In his words, we need to let it help us form a "mental map" of reality that reflects God's own perspective. That mental map will transform our lives and give us a perspective that will help us help the lives of those we serve.

The Bible and Mind Renewal

How can we as leaders keep our minds free from the clutter of conformity to this world? How can we avoid the lies and dangerously subtle half-truths that swirl around us? How do we think about things from the correct perspective?

What we need is what Paul promises in Romans 12:2—a renewed mind.

> Do not conform to the pattern of this world, but be transformed by the renewing of your mind. Then you will be able to test and approve what God's will is—his good, pleasing and perfect will.

One of the most persistent and challenging battles we face is the battle for our minds. When we think correctly, we find success and peace and confidence. But when our thinking is out of whack, everything seems to go awry. Satan's scheme is to try to keep us thinking in our culturally determined, self-centered, and materialistic ways. And he's good at it. But heaven has equipped us with the tools we need to stand against his deceptions.

In Paul's discussion of the armor of God, he instructs his readers to "stand your ground, putting on the belt of truth" (Ephesians 6:14 NLT). When we think about our physical clothing, we know we need something to hold everything together and keep us from exposure to the elements. The spiritual life is the same. We must clothe ourselves in God's truth, because only His truth can defeat all the lies that crowd around us. And we can find that truth in the Scriptures.

Reading the Bible helps us see things differently. It teaches us to reject the lie that says we're unloved…and accept the truth that God loves us unconditionally; to reject the lie that says we always have to defend ourselves…and accept the truth that God is our defender; to reject the lie that says it's all up to us to make things happen…and accept the truth that He's working on our behalf *in His timing*; and to reject the lie that says we have nothing to give…and accept the truth that God has gifted us to serve in our own unique way.

The list could go on and on. And as we study the Scriptures, we can begin to replace all our dark narratives with the light of truth. We're exposed to the Word of God, and our minds are being renewed. Therefore, we must make time in our days for reading, studying, and meditating on Scripture. We can also memorize passages so they'll be right there in our minds when we need them most. Let the Holy Spirit be your teacher as you take a deep dive into the book that is supernaturally powerful. Determine to dredge out your false thinking and replace it with God's truth.

Returning to the food metaphor with which we started this chapter, take the time to let your mind marinate in the Word of God.

Taking Every Thought Captive

During the course of a day, a lot of crazy thoughts make their way into our brains. If we don't pay attention to how we're thinking, if we don't "take captive every thought to make it obedient to Christ" as Paul said in 2 Corinthians 10:5, we can be easily led down the wrong path.

In other words, with all the arguments and ideas that assail us, we're left in a vulnerable place if we just take them in and make them part of our thinking rather than wrestle them into their proper place. They can not only lead us down the wrong path, but sow destruction and result in reckless words and actions. Left unattended, our brains can be dangerous places!

We become what we think, just as our body becomes what it eats. A direct correlation exists between thinking and doing. Sloppy thinking leads to a sloppy way of life, but disciplined thinking leads to a disciplined life. Our minds can be either homes for the Lord or playgrounds for Satan. We need to have the "mind of the Lord" (1 Corinthians 2:16). To achieve this, we must pass through the boot camp of obedience, a place where we'll learn how to take our thoughts captive. Think of it as basic training in thinking, courtesy of God's Word.

Sloppy thinking leads to a sloppy way of life.

Every day we'll be assaulted by atheistic and agnostic arguments that challenge our beliefs. Our worldview will collide with what is accepted by the culture at large. Our values will be rejected as "just another option," and relativism will tell us we can't really be sure that anything is absolutely true. Unless we have steeped our minds in the truth we find in God's Word, we will easily fall prey to these challenges.

Taking thoughts captive isn't just about defending your belief system; it's so much more than that. It's about being obedient to Christ, expressed in an unadulterated commitment to Him. A pure mind grows from our intimate encounters with Jesus. As we spend time

with Him, we learn to think as He thinks, do what He does, go where
He goes, listen to what He listens to, and watch what He watches.

So guard your heart. Guard your eyes. Guard your mind. Don't
capitulate to the siren songs of your unredeemed thoughts. Pay attention to where these thoughts come from and who is whispering them
in your ears. Then reject them. Learn the origin of wrong thinking, and
you can put the thoughts from the Enemy into quarantine.

Instead of allowing your mind to be cluttered with error and neg-
ativity, focus on thoughts that are pure and lovely and wise (Philippians 4:8). Fill your mind with Scripture, and it will seep into your heart.
Let its wisdom empower you as you lead others, always pausing to ask
what Scripture might have to say about the situation at hand.

Soul Care

I've never been much of a gardener. Every year Rita and I set goals
for a healthy and vibrant garden, but we never end up with much of
a harvest. Perhaps instead of a green thumb, I have a black one. I'm
always disappointed when the harvesting season comes around and I
don't have much to show for it. But when I try to evaluate why my garden isn't much of a success, I'm faced with one major reason that stands
above any other: *neglect.*

Both Rita and I have busy lives. So in the midst of work schedules,
being there for our children, grandparenting, and frequent travel during the critical spring and summer months, our poor backyard garden
doesn't get the attention it needs. Even if it begins with a glorious vision,
it soon descends into a weed-ridden mess. Yet my garden needs attention if it's going to thrive and flourish. Unless I'm willing to make it a
priority, it probably isn't going to amount to much. True gardeners are
intentional in doing the hard work.

Our spiritual lives are much like a garden; they need attention and
cultivating to flourish and grow. So like attentive and faithful gardeners, we have to put in the time. We have to pull spiritual and mental
"weeds" so they don't choke out the truth. We need to water and fertilize to keep the soil a good place for growing. We may need to trim
back some unnecessary vines that have entangled us with unhealthy

attachments. If we do all that with a garden—weed, water, fertilize, and trim—we'll have a fruitful garden. And if we do the same kind of things in our spiritual lives, we'll see growth and abundance.

Discipline is necessary for fruitfulness, and one of the most important disciplines is spending time in the Word of God. The Bible is living water that can flood even the most parched and driest soil. Root yourself in that nourished ground. Drink deep of its wisdom.

Spiritually Mature Leaders...

- renew their minds with daily time in the Scriptures,

- are committed to not just believing God's message but living it out in practical ways,

- invite the Holy Spirit to marinate their minds in the Word of God,

- understand the importance of taking every thought captive, and

- tend well the garden of their souls and teach others how to do the same.

CHAPTER 18

MEDITATION

May my meditation be pleasing to him,
as I rejoice in the LORD.

PSALM 104:34

The aim of meditation, in the context of Christian faith, is...
to come to know [God] through the realization that our very
being is penetrated with his knowledge and love for us.

THOMAS MERTON

I f, as we saw in the last chapter, the Word of God is the best guide and source of wisdom for our lives, then we need to not only read it and study it but meditate on it. The wisest people know the power of meditating on God's love as revealed in His Word. They have a passion to hear from Him, which is the goal of meditation. Not to treat the words of Scripture as abstract theological concepts or nifty self-help memes but to ponder, and listen, and learn, and then make changes in our lives.

We need our hearts to be transformed, and nothing will be as effective for that transformation as the kind of listening we do in meditation. When we meditate, we're not looking for more information from the Word's pages, trying to leverage what we've learned for our own advantage, gathering data we can use to impress others or win a Bible trivia quiz. Bible knowledge for its own sake often does little more than promote our pride. No, we're looking for heart transformation.

Sometimes in our relationships with people, we listen to them only so we can size them up. We try to determine how we can persuade them toward our way of thinking, and listening just becomes a lever for personal advantage rather than personal transformation. This doesn't allow us to gather the kind of understanding we need for our spiritual lives and our relationships. But real listening to what God has to say is utterly transformative. It not only helps us become more like Jesus but provides the wisdom every leader needs—wisdom from outside our own enclosed and limited perspectives. Our Master's desire is for us to master meditation for the purpose of His mastery over our lives.

Our Master's desire is for us to master meditation
for the purpose of His mastery over our lives.

But are we, in our heart of hearts, afraid of what Christ might whisper to us when we meditate? Do we hear from Him only what we want to hear? Such selective hearing isn't acceptable to our Savior. Meditation means we pay attention to the full counsel of God. But when you get quiet before Him, are you just trying to get a stamp of approval on what you've already decided? Or a justification for how you're feeling about a situation? Look, you can't pick and choose what you want to appropriate for your life. You have to engage with the challenges and rebukes as well as the whispers of encouragement.

I'm learning that meditation is the quickest path to real spiritual transformation. It unleashes a work of grace in my heart. It's the Spirit's system for governing my daily decisions and grooming me for growth.

When it comes to your life, God doesn't just have some general principles; He has some perfectly tailored plans individually designed for you. He always has a plan, and He has a purpose, but you must quiet yourself to hear them. So dig out some time in your schedule to tap into meditation. Think of the Words of Scripture as letters addressed specifically to you, and then ponder the meanings of what you read and how they might apply to your life right now.

These are not just any letters, though. They're love letters. Read and think on them in that frame of mind. Carve out time for these appointments with God, for they will make you both a better person and the spiritual leader you've always wanted to be.

One of the ways I meditate is by keeping a journal, a written record of what I hear from God. Writing it down, I've found, helps me gain a clearer picture of what's in my heart and how I'm responding. The words expose who I really am and who God really is. Then they provide me with the meat for my meal of meditation. I think and ponder, listen and allow myself to be challenged, then confess and affirm the truth. And I am changed. I can re-read my journal entries later as a reminder of what God has done in my heart.

In meditation, we're looking to experience God at an ever-deepening level.

In meditation, we're looking to experience
Him at an ever-deepening level.

Memory Work Is Heart Work

Those of us who really want to grow in our faith are never satisfied with simply reading the Bible—and certainly not with just having one handy for reference. We want to embed its wisdom and teachings in our hearts, minds, and souls, and the best way to do that is committing Scripture to memory.

Here are four reasons why memorized Scripture is important:

1. *It's perhaps our best tool in the battle against sin, Satan, and self.* When we're in a tight spot or facing a confusing situation, the wisdom of the Word can be instantly brought to bear on what we're going through. When we're tempted by sin, the words we know by heart can help us make the right decision. As the psalmist says, "I have hidden your word in my heart that I might not sin against you" (Psalm 119:11).

2. *It can be used in prayer.* When our hearts are full of gratitude toward God but we don't know how to express it, we can find expression through the Scriptures we've set in our memory. We can say them in prayer.

3. *It provides ready access to God's wisdom.* When we need wisdom, why lean on our own when we have access to God's? We are trained, guided, inspired, and purified by the wisdom from above. Memorizing God's wisdom as given in His Word is one way we can make sure that happens right when we need it.

4. *It can help us witness.* Hiding the Word in our hearts helps us develop the fruit of the Spirit for all to see.

Almost every week, I learn one new verse related to what I'm currently experiencing in my life and my walk with God. That means I store away up to 52 verses every year, so over a period of years I've memorized hundreds of Bible verses to draw on.

Reflect on Christ if You Want to Reflect Him

Our primary goal in our walk with God should be to act as reflectors of Christ in the world. Just as the moon's surface reflects light from the sun, so do we reflect the Son who *is* light. Jesus shines through our souls and reveals Himself in our behavior. His beams of light blanket our lives like the sun's rays warm a sunbather on a hot summer day. God created light (Genesis 1:3), and Jesus called Himself the "light of the world" (John 8:12). He invites us to walk in the greater light of His love, not the lesser light of our own desires and lusts. He wants us to be poster children for His grace.

When reflecting the light of Christ, then, the emphasis should be more on being *like* Jesus than on doing *for* Jesus.

People are drawn to a life that reflects the Lord. And as a leader, you need people to know they can trust you to care about them and that your word can be relied on. All the talk in the world won't accomplish this if your actions don't fit your words. So you let Christ's penetrating light seek out the darkest corners of your life and do the transformative work that allows you to shine for Him.

When we forgive, we reflect Jesus. When we care, we reflect Jesus. When we cry over the condition of someone's soul, we reflect Jesus. When we feed the poor, clothe the naked, administer medical care to the sick, or house the homeless, we reflect Jesus. When we speak a word of encouragement, we reflect Him. When we give generously, we reflect Him. When we are honest, kind, selfless, patient, loving, and good listeners, we reflect Him. When we speak truth with understanding and compassion, we reflect Him.

Bottom line is that the focus of our lives needs to be on reflecting Jesus. We're given the high task of illuminating the world with His light and being His hands and feet to serve others. Where do we get the spiritual power we need to live this way? By feeding ourselves on His Word, where we learn of His person, His character, and His priorities. And the Holy Spirit gives us the wisdom to put these lifegiving words into action.

Contemplating God's Creation

Many theologians agree that God has two books, two ways of communicating with humankind. The first is the Bible, as we've been discussing. The second is His creation. God speaks to us through the beauty, majesty, and mystery of the world in which we live. We can see His fingerprints all over His creation. This is why the psalmist could cry out, "Hallelujah! Praise God in his holy house of worship, praise him under the open skies; praise him for his acts of power, praise him for his magnificent greatness" (Psalm 150:1-2 MSG). We can catch a glimpse of that greatness in the night skies, the soaring mountains, the rushing rivers, the dense forests, the roaring oceans, and in all the creatures He made.

I recently returned from a fly-fishing adventure in South America with a few friends. Located a ten-hour flight south of Atlanta (where I live), Patagonia, Argentina, is spectacular evidence of our Lord's grand, personal presence. This was not only a fishing adventure but a spiritual adventure! What most caught my attention was not the stunning, crystal-clear turquoise rivers and lakes but the dancing light display in the clear night skies overhead. It was hard to find words to describe it, but here is what I wrote in my journal:

> Last night the star-studded sky took my breath away. Like gazing up at a domed planetarium, I was mesmerized by my Master's magnificence. Praise Him under the open skies! The black backdrop was blanketed with a diverse array of diamond clustered stars, planets, and celestial creations that only our Creator could have arranged with such striking display of grandeur. The Southern Cross, visible only in the Southern Hemisphere, offered no hint of disappointment on my first gaze upward at this heavenly canvas. Orion's inspiring symmetry contrasted with the asymmetrical cluster of mystery we call the Milky Way. God's grand design marched across the sky with a silent shout of "Hallelujah to Him!" An orange comet streaked past…Praise Him for His acts of power, praise Him for His magnificent greatness.

The heavens are declaring the glory of God, and the skies are proclaiming the work of His hands. They have no "voice," yet they speak of His majesty (Psalm 119:1). I've learned I need to listen to what God is revealing through the world He created. When I meditate on His greatness, He becomes bigger and I become smaller. I understand my place in a wider and bigger plan.

I also think about David, who wrote so many of the psalms. While a shepherd, he watched over his flocks on the hillside of his homeland or beside still waters. Every night, once the sheep were safely secured, he was free to spend hours gazing up at the grandeur of God's creation. In such moments, his faith grew into that of a fearless giant-killer.

So listen to the Word and meditate on it. Look up at the world around you and listen for God to speak there too. Make room in your life for an occasional getaway into the wild, somewhere away from the hubbub of our culture, where you can listen to God speaking in riotous beauty, in the gentle whisper of the wind, in the song of a bird, or in the lapping of sea waves. It'll remind you of who you worship and why. It'll give you something to meditate on.

Let God love you both in front of the open Book and under the open sky.

Spiritually Mature Leaders...

- store up God's Word in their hearts so it might guide, comfort, encourage, and transform them,

- understand that memorized Scripture is a powerful weapon in the battle against sin,

- strive to be a reflection of Christ as they follow Christ's words and actions,

- allow the light of God to penetrate into the darkest corners of their lives, and

- contemplate God's greatness in the beauty and majesty of the created world.

CHAPTER 19

SOLITUDE AND SILENCE

*In repentance and rest is your salvation, in
quietness and trust is your strength.*

Isaiah 30:15

*There is a pleasure in the pathless woods,
There is a rapture on the lonely shore,
There is society, where none intrudes,
By the deep sea, and music in its roar;
I love not Man the less, but Nature more.*

Lord Byron

We live in a noisy world, and it can be hard to get away from all the distraction that presses on our attention. Sometimes I just want to take a vacation from my cell phone, email, and all the other technology that's supposed to make my life more efficient but is often intrusive to my peace of mind. If I don't control my technology, it will control me.

What a blessing to know that no matter how complicated life becomes, God has given us an invitation to a different way of living: "Be still, and know that I am God" (Psalm 46:10). In other words, amid all the chaos and noise of life, we can go to Him, not through a lot of passionate or eloquent words but in simple silence and stillness. When we leave the world behind, we find Him there. He awaits us and invites us to enter into His quiet.

In her helpful book *Invitation to Solitude and Silence*, Ruth Haley Barton offers these profound thoughts:

> The invitation to solitude and silence is . . . an invitation to enter more deeply into the intimacy of relationship with the One who waits just outside the noise and busyness of our lives. It is an invitation to communication and communion with the One who is always present even when our awareness has been dulled by distraction. It is an invitation into the adventure of spiritual transformation into the deepest places of our being, an adventure that will result in greater and greater freedom and authenticity and surrender to God than we have yet experienced.[13]

Barton is surely right that silence can make us nervous. Not only are most of us unused to it, but we try to keep ourselves busy so we don't have to face...us. When we commune with God in silence, we're forced to commune with our own hearts, to be honest about our failures and what we don't like about ourselves. And when there's a lull in conversation with a friend or coworker, we tend to want to say something—*anything*—to fill the silent void that makes us so uncomfortable. When we approach God, we also feel we must say something—explain, confess, or make an excuse.

Honest communication with God in solitude and silence means coming to the end of ourselves. It means admitting that what we've tried in order to control our lives and satiate the thirst in our souls hasn't worked. That's why God isn't always looking for words. Sometimes He just wants to allow us the pleasure of simply being with Him and letting Him love us.

Honest communication with God in solitude and silence means coming to the end of ourselves.

In silence, we come to a crisis of choice. We can stop running frantically from this promise of happiness to the next one, from this false god to that one, and settle at our Master's feet—the only place our souls can truly find rest. Or we can continue to pretend we aren't desperate and miss out on the transformative power of spending time alone with God.

Quiet and Still...and Content

The author of Psalm 131 knew the power of calm and quiet to change his heart: "I do not concern myself with great matters...I have calmed and quieted myself, I am like a weaned child with its mother; like a weaned child I am content" (verses 1-2). A mother is always a comfort to her child, even as he ages, forever helping him be content because he knows she's continually ready to give him what he needs from her.

So it is with us and God. He is forever our comfort. And though we may not always get what we *want* as we linger quietly with Him, we can be content in anticipation because we know we'll get what we *need* in His time. You may want to leave, but He knows you need to stay. You may want to start a business, but He knows you need to focus on ministry. You may want to marry, but He knows you need to wait until your life is in better order. You may want a promotion, but He knows you need to learn to be faithful right where you are. And the Holy Spirit may actually be weaning you off something or someone, so prepare your heart for the future in silent waiting.

God wants you to know that all you *really* need is Him. So still and quiet your soul by inviting your heavenly Father's warm embrace to encircle you. You will be content and sleep well when He holds you.

By God's grace, remain childlike in your faith and character. Jesus said, "Unless you change and become like little children, you will never enter the kingdom of heaven" (Matthew 18:3). So keep your heart humble and honest under heaven's hope. Look to God for comfort and security, for confidence and strength. Rest in silence, where you can best experience His embrace, and let your soul be settled.

The raging waves of the world's worries crash against the shore of our souls:

A missed deadline.

A bad financial decision.

A communication breakdown.

A rebellious child.

Failure at school.

Depression at how alone we feel.

All these loud problems tend to deafen our ears to the quiet whisper of peace God wants to speak to us.

Has a temporary tempest in your trust caused you to tread lightly into the Lord's presence? Are you afraid that the winds of adversity blow too hard to continue to bear them? Just as Jesus calmed a storm as His boat was tossed about by the waves, so He will calm our crisis when we feel buffeted about and are taking on water. He is still in control, and He can always be trusted. He said, "In this world you will have trouble. But take heart! I have overcome the world" (John 16:33).

Whatever you may be going through—take heart! The One who has overcome the world will meet you in the quiet place there in the eye of the storm. As the old hymn says, while "the sea billows blow," you can still find the confidence to say, "It is well with my soul." The presence of Jesus awaits the hungry heart that does not give up on God. Whatever the situation, go to Him. Only in silence can our souls be resuscitated by the Savior. He will work wonders in us if we wait before Him. He can speak calm and contentment into our personal storms.

If you think you don't have time to be alone with God, that confirms you're too busy with your own agenda. Especially as one who leads others, you need to be led by Him. As one who needs to comfort others, you need to be comforted by Him. As one who often needs to calm an out-of-control situation, you need to know His calm. What you learn in silence and solitude will give you the ability to bring others to a place of peace and calm as well.

Wait in Silence for God

What are we supposed to do in silence? Perhaps we first need to get honest about the state of our souls. Confession breaks down the walls of separation and purifies us to enter His presence. We don't have to be perfect when we go before God, but we must be honest—honest with ourselves, and more importantly, honest with Him. His forgiveness is the key to entering fully into His presence.

And then we wait.

"O my soul," the psalmist instructs himself, "wait in silence, for my hope is from him" (Psalm 62:5 ESV). The context for this psalm is this: it was written by someone who felt like he kept getting kicked when he was already down for the count. I think all of us, at one time or another, can relate. Sometimes we reach seasons of life when the entire deck seems stacked against us, where confusion and pain seem to be waiting around every corner and in the middle of each situation.

This particular psalm speaks to us all when we feel that way. The verse above is the cry of someone who is desperate for peace and eager for hope. When the psalmist reaches the end of his rope, he finds the prescription for what ails his heart. In fact, he speaks these words to himself as a command. He's talking to himself and reminding himself of what he really needs to do. (This is a good reminder that talking to yourself isn't always the sign of a crazy person. Sometimes telling ourselves the larger truth about life is exactly what we need!)

Finding stillness and silence begins with becoming aware of the degree of unrest and conflict we're facing. If we're lost in the chaos of life, we might not even be aware of how far we've strayed from peace. We can't find peace if we don't acknowledge the unrest. The psalmist isn't suggesting that we wait for the day when everything feels settled in the world, when we're carefree and lighthearted, to go to the Lord in solitude and silence. No, the challenge is for us to go when we feel overworked and underpaid. When we're embroiled in an argument with our spouse or in a disagreement with our superiors that just seems to stretch on and on. When we feel like a failure as a parent. When we're facing a life-threatening health issue. Or when we actually doubt the goodness or nearness of God.

These are the moments when we must be still and wait in silence. In the places of pain, God asks us to wait on Him, trusting that He is present in the chaos and will speak the needed order, hope, and peace into our hearts. The best spiritual leaders follow Jesus in the process of learning to be still in the midst of the chaos.

The best spiritual leaders follow Jesus
in the process of learning to be still
in the midst of the chaos.

Linger Longer with the Lord

Let's look again at Psalm 46:10 and add verse 11: "Be still, and know that I am God…the LORD Almighty is with us." An important part of silence and solitude is learning to take the time to, in the old phrase, *tarry* with the Lord. But to get the most out of such personal times of intimacy with God, we can't be in a hurry to finish and move on to the next thing on our list. We must allow the necessary time for our souls to be slowly bathed in love and peace and our spiritual ears to hear a fresh reminder of God's call on our lives.

The older I get, the longer I want to linger with good people and good times. I used to rush from place to place, from person to person, from experience to experience. I always needed to be doing something else, and that kept me moving. But now I've learned to luxuriate in the moments I'm given.

Not long ago I spent a weekend with a group of guys (the fourteenth year of doing so) at a friend's cabin on the cusp of the mountains of northern Georgia. We spent unhurried time among the timber-laden hills, where we didn't have any real agenda. It was a time for inhaling the goodness of God among the Georgia pines and being emotionally healed as we spent time both alone and together, just seeking God. We laughed, we cried, and we listened to the voice of God whispering on the wind. We lingered long with each other, and we lingered long with God.

What does it mean to be still and know our creator? Much more than a motionless body, an inner stillness serenades the soul with tranquility so that the cares of the world lose their caustic control. The great Divine Artist wants us to sit at His feet and watch Him add brush strokes of His brilliance to our personal stories, creating something out of the nothing in our lives. We have to sit still so He can work on His masterpieces—on you and me. We dare not rush away before He's finished His artistry.

Other people may have insights to offer, but the wisdom that makes for the most profound change can be found at the feet of Jesus. You and I have an ever-present Helper waiting for us to seek His face in trust. The fruit of a frantic pace is anxiety, but the fruit of faith is peace. Linger with the Lord to enjoy the good fruit of intimacy with Him.

What appointment could be more important than meeting with your Maker? What investment of time is more valuable than time spent with Him? What experience is more lifegiving than sitting quietly and absorbing His love for you? How do children feel when they're invited to crawl into the lap of a parent to find security and affection? Like those children are invited by moms and dads, we are invited into the lap of our Lord. To linger there and enjoy His presence and gather the strength we need to face whatever the day may bring our way. Spiritually mature leaders learn to linger longer with the Lord and abide in the depths of His rich love.

Spiritually mature leaders learn to
linger longer with the Lord and abide
in the depths of His rich love.

Hebrews 4:10-11 tells us, "Anyone who enters God's rest also rests from their works, just as God did from his. Let us, therefore, make every effort to enter that rest."

Spiritually Mature Leaders...

- understand the importance of times of silence and solitude with God,

- develop the kind of "eye-of-the-storm" calm they can bring to bear on every crisis,

- find the resources to carry on in their quiet times with God,

- embrace a childlike trust in God, and

- linger longer with the Lord.

CHAPTER 20

SELF-DENIAL

*Whoever wants to be my disciple must deny themselves
and take up their cross daily and follow me.*

LUKE 9:23

*There is only one thing which is generally
safe from plagiarism—self-denial.*

G.K. CHESTERTON

The words of Jesus above, where He talks about denying ourselves and taking up our cross, are hard for us to hear. We want to follow Jesus, but most of us aren't excited about the idea that following Him might result in pain and suffering. As human beings, we spend a lot of time and energy on figuring out how to alleviate or eradicate suffering. Or even better, we want to know how to avoid it entirely. The last thing we want to do is embrace misery. We visit doctors, take medication, and chase the latest fad diets, all in the hope of living a healthy, pain-free existence. We assume that if something is painful or uncomfortable, it must be bad and should be banished or never encountered at all.

In all honesty, too often we tend to apply this same reasoning to our spiritual lives. We assume—or at least we want to believe—that the Christian life is meant to be pleasant and pain-free, with God lavishing blessing after blessing on us. Then when it isn't pleasant and pain-free, we assume our faith must somehow be lacking or we've yet to master some spiritual secret. We've bought into this version of Christianity because we've convinced ourselves that our faith is about conforming God into our image rather than conforming ourselves into His.

By nature, we're wired for selfish gain, comfortable living, and pain-free indulgence. By grace, however, we're invited into a radically different way of living—the way of the cross. This path turns away from self-love and self-concern and embraces the challenge of living the Christlike life even when it's painful and costs us our comfort or security. When Jesus asks us to follow Him, we must remember where His journey led.

Dietrich Bonhoeffer, the modern-day martyr executed by the Nazi regime, famously described the way of the believer this way: "When Christ calls a man, he bids him come and die."[14]

The Christian life is an invitation into daily self-denial, putting to death our own "rights" to pleasure or self-gain. It's an invitation to die to our old selves in order to learn what it means to be truly alive. This is the paradoxical heart of the Christian message—through death we find life. Although it can be painful to live for Christ and not for ourselves, we must trust that it *is* the only way to find real and lasting joy, peace, and happiness.

Romans 6:8 tells us, "Now if we died with Christ, we believe that we will also live with him."

This is the paradoxical heart of the Christian message—through death we find life.

Nothing You Give Up for Christ Is Lost

Years ago, married with children, I felt God's nudge to relocate to a new city. I was excited about the opportunity to attend graduate school, and because my family never stayed in one place too long as I was growing up, the thought of our moving to a city far away was no big deal for me. I was a little like Abraham, ready to go wherever God called.

But the move was pretty hard for Rita. She grieved about being that far from her extended family. They were so important to her, and she struggled with the change. But she was onboard. She was willing to give up proximity to them so we could pursue a different ministry path.

But to be honest, once the initial excitement of making the move began to fade, I started to worry a little. In fact, I found myself weeping with uncertainty. In a moment when I was crying out to God (literally crying!), He led me to Acts 18:9-11, a passage that somewhat paralleled my own situation:

> One night the Lord spoke to Paul in a vision, "Do not be afraid; keep on speaking, do not be silent. For I am with you, and no one is going to attack and harm you, because I have many people in this city." So Paul stayed in Corinth for a year and a half, teaching them the word of God.

This was just the encouragement I needed. I didn't have to feel fearful or alone. I knew God had led us to this season of trust, service, and education, and Rita and I grew even closer together through this challenging time. Looking back, it was an important period of preparation for the years to come, and our sacrifice eventually opened many doors for ministry.

Every sacrifice for Jesus Christ will be ultimately redeemed. God takes nothing from us without providing, in time, a multiplied restoration in a new and glorious form. Seen from this perspective, my challenges take on a different meaning. I know that in the long run, God will rescue, restore, and redeem me. Everything I have lost translates to something new I will find.

Such a conviction is why Corrie ten Boom, the beloved author and speaker, was able to survive the horrors of a concentration camp. Her time in that horrifying place taught her the limited worth of earthly treasures and the value of the joy that's eternal. Corrie stood at the very door of death, and when she did, heaven's priorities became illuminated.

We gain a life-changing interior freedom when we realize that no earthly thing will ever be able to destroy us. Nothing can ruin us. No disappointment will keep us down. Nothing we give up for Jesus is lost. Therefore, we need to invest our lives in things that have an eternal reward. In Matthew 6:19-20, Jesus said, "Do not lay up for yourselves treasures on earth, where moth and rust destroy and where thieves break in and steal, but lay up for yourselves treasures in heaven, where neither moth nor rust destroys and where thieves do not break in and steal" (ESV).

Nothing we give up for Jesus is lost.

Bearing the Cross

In the days of Christ's time on earth, the cross was Rome's ultimate instrument of death. Hanging there was an almost unthinkably horrific way to die. But Jesus submitted Himself to this way of death to earn life for us. When I take up my cross, I'm choosing a hard path, but I'm choosing one that leads to eternal glory. If I'm not willing to bear the cross, I can't really be called a disciple. The cost of discipleship is death to my old, sinful self, and the promise of discipleship is the joyful reality of embodying Christ's resurrected life. For Jesus, the cross and the tomb were followed by resurrection and glory.

When I bear my cross, I might have to give up what I want in order to meet someone else's needs. Perhaps I'll have to give up a cool opportunity so someone else can enjoy the unique experience. I might have to give up travel for work so I'm more available to my family. I might have to give up buying a new car, instead providing a good used one for someone who needs it. And as a leader, I might have to give up a wage increase so poorly paid employees can earn more, or I might need to sacrifice my time to train or encourage others or even help them finish a project.

The sacrifices we make show our willingness to bear the burdens of others.

Sometimes the cross you bear may have you feeling as though you're near a breaking point. The pain might seem too heavy, and you may feel crushed under the weight of worry, weakness, and a need for relief. You might feel rejected, misunderstood, and forgotten. But always remember that Jesus has already walked this difficult path, and He has not forgotten you. He suffered, died, and rose again *for you*, so that your broken heart could be healed by His grace, your burden of shame could be lifted by His love, and your loneliness could be filled by His precious presence. He is the ultimate burden bearer, and you never bear your burdens alone.

Fasting

One of the most powerful ways to train in self-denial is through fasting—setting aside a period of time to deny ourselves food. Fasting flushes toxins from our system, and a break from solid food can wean us from its addictive influence. (What consumes us, controls us.) But when we take even 24 hours to say no to food, we can recalibrate our spiritual desires along with our earthly ones.

An article from the Leadership Ministries, Inc. website tells us this about fasting:

> Fasting was an established practice in the time of Christ (Matthew 9:14-15; Mark 2:18-20; Luke 5:33-35) and was also practiced in the early church. Fasting is a voluntary activity, not a forced activity. During fasting, the blood in your body used for digestive processes or exercise is available to the brain for increased mental exercise. For this reason fasting is an opportunity to increase your spiritual alertness as you study and pray while abstaining from meals.[15]

Before you launch into a fast, it's important to learn more about how to do it, and this article also shares some tips. You need to understand how to approach your fast, especially if you're doing it for the first time.

Below are four further purposes of fasting that same article shows we can find in Scripture. The words are a direct quote, but I've presented them with bullet points.

1. *To overcome temptation*

   • Jesus Christ was led to fast for 40 days (Matthew 4:2).

2. *To seek God's will in a specific matter*

   • The Israelites fasted to determine direction in battle (Judges 20:26).

   • Paul and Barnabas prayed and fasted before choosing elders (Acts 14:23).

3. *To repent from sin*

   • The Israelites fasted as they repented and put away false gods (1 Samuel 7:6).

   • David fasted and repented of sin (2 Samuel 12:16 and 12:23).

   • Daniel fasted and repented for himself and the people for not having walked in the laws of the Lord (Daniel 9:3).

   • The people of Nineveh repented and fasted (Jonah 3:5).

(I'm adding three more examples: Ahab fasted and repented after causing Naboth's death [1 Kings 21:27]; hearing God's Word, Israel fasted, confessing their sins [Nehemiah 9:1-3]; and Joel called for a fast because of the Lord's chastening [Joel 1:14; 2:12,15].)

4. *To increase concern for the work of God*

   • Nehemiah fasted over the condition of Jerusalem (Nehemiah 1:4).

If we're going to fast, we should not only proceed with caution but with the right frame of mind. I think John Wesley addressed both. First, his caution:

Let us beware…of fancying we merit anything of God by our fasting. We cannot be too often warned of this; inasmuch as a desire to "establish our own righteousness," to procure salvation of debt and not of grace, is so deeply rooted in all our hearts. Fasting is only a way which God hath ordained, wherein we wait for his unmerited mercy; and wherein, without any desert of ours, he hath promised freely to give us his blessing.[16]

And then this guideline:

First, let [fasting] be done unto the Lord, with our eye singly fixed on Him. Let our intention herein be this, and this alone, to glorify our Father which is in heaven; to express our sorrow and shame for our manifold transgressions of his holy law; to wait for an increase of purifying grace, drawing our affections to things above; to add seriousness and earnestness to our prayers; to avert the wrath of God; and to obtain all the great and precious promises which He hath made to us in Jesus Christ.[17]

The discipline of occasional fasting will bear powerful fruit in your spiritual life and be a source for obtaining the wisdom and spiritual maturity you need to be an effective leader.

Spiritually Mature Leaders...

- know self-denial leads to spiritual freedom,

- take up their cross daily to follow the way of the Savior,

- understand the difference between earthly and heavenly priorities,

- believe that what is lost for Christ is gained for eternity, and

- fast to recalibrate their spiritual desires and draw closer to Christ.

CHAPTER 21

DRESSED FOR SUCCESS: SPIRITUAL WARFARE

Now my beloved ones, I have saved these most important truths for last: Be supernaturally infused with strength through your life-union with the Lord Jesus. Stand victorious with the force of his explosive power flowing in and through you.

<small>EPHESIANS 6:10 TPT</small>

Pick up your God-given weapons...learn to wage victorious spiritual warfare using divinely provided weapons. Only then will you experience the thrill of victory rather than the agony of defeat.

<small>TONY EVANS</small>

Any person or any leader who decides to follow the path of deepening their spiritual life will quickly find that it isn't just a matter of trying to do all the right things. No matter how hard we attempt to live with purity and integrity, we always seem to come up against resistance. That resistance isn't just a psychological hang-up; it's a spiritual force against which we are doing battle. If you aren't engaged in this battle for your soul, you will not find the peace and victory promised by Jesus.

C.S. Lewis once said that the most effective strategy of the enemy of our souls is to get us to doubt his existence. Some people just aren't really tuned into the spiritual realm, and they see everything only through an earthly perspective. Others dismiss the existence of the devil, considering him a myth. In either case, those who don't comprehend the existence of a real being who is evil are doomed to be manipulated by him.

When we're oblivious to Satan's wiles, we are captive to his power. We'll never experience the abundant life God wants to give us if we're lost in the maze of the Enemy's territory. We need to be aware of the existence of a supernatural realm, realizing that choices in one realm have consequences in the other. Many people are poorly prepared to do battle with Satan because they're too busy to pay attention to anything except what's right in front of them. And so they fall victim to temptation and misdirection and error.

We need to be prepared for this battle. Our preparation will determine how much victory we experience and how effectively we can help lead others enmeshed in similar spiritual struggles. In Ephesians 6:12, Paul reminds us that our biggest battles in life are ultimately spiritual: "Our struggle is not against flesh and blood, but against the rulers, against the authorities, against the powers of this dark world and against the spiritual forces of evil in the heavenly realms." We are waging a war every day against the devil and his demons.

Sometimes Satan can be heard coming, as he sometimes roars like a lion. Other times he may sneak up on us like a slithering snake, cold and deadly and sly. If we don't learn to recognize his ways, we will fall prey to his machinations. That's why Paul next talks about the spiritual armor we desperately need to engage in this battle:

> Put on the full armor of God to protect yourselves from the devil and his evil schemes. We're not waging war against enemies of flesh and blood alone. No, this fight is against tyrants, against authorities, against supernatural powers and demon princes that slither in the darkness of this world, and against wicked spiritual armies that lurk about in heavenly places (Ephesians 6:11-12 THE VOICE).

The question we must ask ourselves is this: *Am I at the mercy of the devil's schemes, or am I prepared with the weaponry I need to fight against his lies?* When we look at the various elements of armor Paul goes on to discuss in Ephesians 6, we see they involve not only defensive weapons but the offensive weapons we need to take the battle to the devil. We don't have to just wait in fear; we can launch out to achieve victory. Effective spiritual leaders are on the offensive with praise and prayer—and on the defensive by preparing themselves with the whole armor of God.

Effective spiritual leaders are on the offensive with praise and prayer—and on the defensive by preparing themselves with the whole armor of God.

The most powerful weapon the Enemy has is his lies. If he can get us to believe what isn't true—about God, our lives, our friends and families, and ourselves—then he can manipulate us effectively. We must not trust or depend on our own power or try to fight him in our own strength. We need to use the weapons God provides: faith and truth and His Word. The power of God's love chases down the devil and casts away our feelings of fear and inadequacy. And when our minds and hearts are filled with truth, with God's reality, there's no room for the father of lies, as Jesus calls him in John 8:44.

I hope you can sense Paul's urgency when he wrote, "The night is nearly over; the day is almost here. So let us put aside the deeds of darkness and put on the armor of light" (Romans 13:12).

The Full Armor

When our daughters were children, they sometimes raced outside into the cold in the very dead of winter wearing only a short-sleeved shirt—and no gloves, no jacket, no scarf, no hat! They didn't want to take the time to prepare themselves with all that heavy clothing. Anticipating the fun they were going to have made them too impatient to take the time to dress warmly. Consequently, they never lasted long in the frigid air. Eventually, they learned it was better to be patient and let Rita or me help them dress appropriately.

That's what Paul was encouraging the Christians of his day to do in Ephesians 6:14-17: dress appropriately, and dress for success. He knew everyone was aware of how the Roman soldiers were attired, so he used their gear as the model for the spiritual soldiers who needed to always be ready to do battle. No soldier would run into battle without the proper equipment. He wouldn't go into combat without a sword, a shield, a helmet to protect his head, and proper footwear. Without these, he would be at a disadvantage when he fought hand to hand with an opponent.

Similarly, we need to make sure we gear up to take on our spiritual antagonist. By faith, we suit up in the spiritual armor God has requisitioned for us. His weapons, when used properly, are lethal against any enemy attack.

Sometimes we're tempted to fight these battles with our own resources—our strength, wisdom, and intelligence. But this is always a mistake. Our own strengths and abilities are not adequate to the task. In 2 Corinthians 10:3-5, Paul wrote,

> We are human, but we don't wage war as humans do. We use God's mighty weapons, not worldly weapons, to knock down the strongholds of human reasoning and to destroy false arguments. We destroy every proud obstacle that keeps people from knowing God. We capture their rebellious thoughts and teach them to obey Christ (NLT).

We can't just grit our teeth and will away our temptations. We can't just talk ourselves out of dangerous ideas and plans. We can't reason our way out of a rough patch. And we can't allow ourselves to think only about self-preservation. When we do that, we play right into the devil's hands.

As leaders, we need to be cautious about trusting too much in our own wisdom and experience. We need God's perspective. And sometimes getting God's perspective on a situation necessitates battling back all our own thinking and the lies we've come to believe. We need to lean into the Lord's weapons of faith, truth, righteousness, and loving salvation.

Victory is assured, but only if we do battle alongside the Captain of our souls.

Tempered by Truth

When I was younger, I often took the wrong approach to my challenges. Whether involving relationships, work, family, church, or my connection with the Lord, I tended to be a mile wide and an inch deep in every endeavor. I usually tried to do my best and work hard, but I was working beyond the capacity of my limited experience with God. I had to learn, and I'm still learning, how to let the Spirit of Truth lead me. That sometimes means saying no to what seems like a good opportunity, but timing is everything.

Truth will always be available; I just need to be available to truth. Truth is the ultimate weapon against the devil's lies. We need the belt of truth firmly fastened around our waists if we are to stand our ground against the evil one (Ephesians 6:14). And we need the sword of the Word to cut through all the lies that surround us. Sharp is the discernment that comes from knowing the Word, a weapon of great precision. It's so razor-sharp that it's always accurate, revealing the depths of motivation and desire. It helps us harness our emotions so they can be led by truth—set free to express pure love, joy, peace, patience, and kindness, all fruit of the Spirit. If we fill our minds with God's Word, we fill our minds with truth.

Will you let your mind marinate in God's truths? Just as when you prepare a delicious entrée and then take the time to cover it with seasoning and let it simmer? But in this case, you season your thoughts with Christ's wisdom. Then you let His truths simmer as long as needed so your soul can feast on them.

You need to be prepared to go into battle. You need your full armor and a prepared heart. That means every day should hold a routine of developing battle readiness. Sit with your Savior, immerse yourself in His Word, pray with your heart, and listen with your spirit. When this becomes the central time of each day, you'll be a better soldier, prepared to help others, battle false ideas, and lead God's charge for your own life and the lives of others.

Effective spiritual leaders understand that a little bit of daily preparation goes a long way in renewing their minds with the truth that brings freedom from Satan's ploys.

Spiritually Mature Leaders...

- understand that life is a battle against an unseen enemy,

- learn that Satan comes like a roaring lion *and* like a slithering snake,

- daily clothe themselves in the full complement of God's armor,

- know that spiritual battles cannot be fought with human resources, and

- embrace the Bible as the sword of the Spirit that cuts through lies and deception.

Stormie Omartian is a prayer warrior. I doubt anyone in our contemporary times has had a greater impact on leading people in how to pray. Her books have sold more than 40 million copies and challenged readers to seek God in every area of their lives.

I sat down with Stormie to talk about spiritual leadership, and these are some of my favorite thoughts she shared in that conversation:

> [When I was] a fairly new Christian, my church asked me and my husband, Michael, to start a small group. In addition to our weekly meetings, we added a prayer meeting once a month where we focused only on praying together. Michael would take the men in the living room to pray, and I would take the women in our bedroom, where we sat in a circle to pray. Every time, there were so many prayer requests that we would often pray until one o'clock in the morning. People were that hungry for prayer. They wanted to be prayed *for*, and they also wanted to pray *with* and *for others* too. That's how our prayer groups for marriages, children, emotional healing, and personal ministry began, and that's where eventually the inspiration for all of my prayer books came from.

I believe in the power of praying together—even with just one other person. The power of prayer increases exponentially when we do that. So if you can join—or put together—a small prayer group, you will see how the power of praying together cannot be denied. Other people see that; they feel it. That's why people attended these prayer groups so faithfully, because they could express their needs and be prayed for specifically. It was remarkable to see God's power move in response to our prayers.

————

It's important to be right before God all the time, every day, so before I pray, I say to God, *"Lord, if there's something I need to confess to You, bring it to my mind. Show me."* The truth is, we can all do less than the right thing and not realize it until God brings it to our mind. For example, He might reveal an unkind attitude you had with a person. Or perhaps you could have handled something differently. It is not condemnation; it is conviction. And confession is always important, because if we don't acknowledge before God our less than perfect attitudes or actions, the enemy can find a way into our heart. It says in the Bible, "If I regard iniquity in my heart, the Lord will not listen." It's not like He can't listen; it's that He will not listen to your prayer until your heart is right. Sometimes we're waiting on the Lord, and He's waiting for us to go before Him and say, *"I humble myself before You, Lord. Reveal to me anything that I need to confess to You. Show me anything I must do or stop doing."*

————

The Lord is kind. He doesn't pour condemnation on us. That's the work of the enemy, who wants to make us feel guilty about everything that we do, and, as a result, we always feel bad about ourselves. God wants you to feel good about what He's put in you and all that He is doing in you. God is good, and He wants us to clear up anything that gets in the way of the high purpose He has for your life.

————

Sometimes you may feel as if your prayers are going three inches up and then falling to the ground, as opposed to flying up to heaven. But that comes from your own doubts or lack of knowledge about God and His ways. The truth is, God hears your prayers. Sometimes He answers in ways you're not expecting, but you have to trust that God knows what's best for you. He hears your prayers. He's listening. Your prayers are making a difference—even when you think they're not reaching Him. Don't beat yourself up when you feel too tired, exhausted, or worried to even pray. Go ahead and take it all to Him. Even if you just sit before Him and sing a worship song. Don't worry about what your voice sounds like; He doesn't care. He looks at your heart. He hears what your heart is saying. He loves you and will answer those prayers. But you have to let Him be God, trusting He will answer in His way and time.

Every time you read the Bible, you're learning something new, even when you read the same passage you read just a week ago. It's like a new Bible every time you read it because you've learned so much in the past week that now you have new insight and God's showing you deeper things. So you can never stop reading the Bible because you never stop learning from it. God's Word will change your life when you ask Him to reveal new things to you as you read.

The busier I get, the more dependent I am on God, because I cannot get through the day without spending time with Him in worship, in prayer, and in His Word. If you are not connected to God right from the beginning of your day, you're going to have a harder time accomplishing everything you need to get done. It is better to establish your dependence upon the Lord as early in the day as possible and say, "*God, You know I can't do anything meaningful or lasting without You. I worship You because You are great and mighty and there is nothing too hard for You. You are my peace and my joy, and I depend on You for my strength.*"

When you are certain you can't take one step without Him, then you know for sure that every step you take guided by Him will lead you in the right direction. Show your dependence on Him by saying, "*God, guide me in this. Teach me how to do the right thing. Show me how to pray in this situation. Help me make the right decisions. Show me what to do.*"

———

Jesus said, "Where two or more are gathered in My name, I'm there." If you pray with even one other person, the Lord promises to be there with you in greater measure. Sometimes you have to pray and pray about something, but don't give up. Eventually you will see an answer to that prayer.

Ask God to bring someone into your life who's a strong believer and who wants to pray with you. When He shows you someone, be brave and ask that person, "*Would you be willing to pray together with me once a week?*" And if they say no, don't be concerned about that. Some people are not ready to pray with someone else. It just means that they are not the right one for you. Keep looking and asking. There will be someone who says yes, and you will be glad they did.

A PRAYER FOR YOU
TO PRAY AS A
SPIRITUAL LEADER

We've covered a lot of territory in this book, and I hope it's given you some insights and tools to help you grow spiritually stronger and become the kind of spiritual leader you've always wanted to be. You might need to revisit some chapters now and then as they become especially relevant to your needs, but it has been an honor to share my heart with you on these important topics.

I'd like to close with a prayer for you to pray as a spiritual leader—and pray often.

> *Gracious God, loving Father, forgiving Son, comforting Spirit,*
> *You have called me to love You, and I love You with all my being.*
> *You have called me to follow You, and I humbly follow and obey You.*
> *You have called me to worship You, and I praise*
> *and worship You with my whole heart.*
> *You have called me to trust You, and I have*
> *total trust and faith in You.*
> *You have called me to ask You for wisdom,*
> *and I seek You for the wise thing to do.*
> *You have called me to serve You, and I faithfully serve You.*
>
> *You also call me to love others; help me lay down my life for them.*
> *You call me to serve others; help me serve them selflessly.*

You call me to comfort others; help me be present to grieve with them.
You call me to rejoice with others; help me rejoice in grateful celebration.
You call me to pray for others; help me to pray boldly and often for them.
You call me to lead others; help me be a leader worth following.

In Jesus's name,
amen.

NOTES

1. Oswald Chambers, *The Love of God* (Grand Rapids, MI: Discovery House Publishers, 1988), 67.

2. *American Dictionary of the English Language,* http://webstersdictionary1828.com/Dictionary/abide.

3. Andrew Murray, *Abide in Christ: The Joy of Being in God's Presence* (New Kensington, PA: Whitaker House), 38.

4. Henri J.M. Nouwen, *The Way of the Heart* (New York: Ballantine Books, 1983), 21.

5. Henri J.M. Nouwen, *Our Second Birth* (New York: Crossroads, 2006), 132-133.

6. Shauna Schutte, "Peacemakers Forgive First," https://www.wisdomhunters.com/peacemakers-forgive-first/.

7. Patrick Morley, *The Christian Man* (Grand Rapids, MI: Zondervan, 2019), 91.

8. Pope Francis with Antonio Spadrado, *My Door Is Always Open* (London: Bloomsbury, 2014), 54.

9. Henri J.M. Nouwen, *The Return of the Prodigal Son* (New York: Crown Publishing Group, 2013), 85.

10. Elizabeth Gilbert, *Eat, Pray, Love* (New York: Penguin, 2007), 60.

11. Charles Spurgeon, "The Golden Alphabet," https://www.spurgeongems.org/chs_golden-alphabet.pdf.

12. Dallas Willard, *Living in Christ's Presence* (Downers Grove, IL: InterVarsity Press, 2013), 61.

13. Ruth Haley Barton, *Invitation to Solitude and Silence* (Downers Grove, IL: InterVarsity Press, 2010), 16.

14. Dietrich Bonhoeffer, *The Cost of Discipleship* (New York: Touchstone, 1995), 14.

15. "A Fast Quickens the Spirit," https://leadmin.org/articles/2018/5/17/a-fast-quickens-the-spirit?rq=fast.

16. John Wesley, sermon 27, "Upon Our Lord's Sermon On The Mount: Discourse Seven," section IV, No. 2, https://nnu.whdl.org/sites/default/files/publications/EN_John_Wesley_023_sermon_on_the_mount_7.pdf.

17. John Wesley, sermon 27, section IV, No. 1, https://nnu.whdl.org/sites/default/files/publications/EN_John_Wesley_023_sermon_on_the_mount_7.pdf .

BIBLE NOTIFICATIONS

Rita graduated from Gadsden State Jr. College with a Medical Lab Tech associates degree in 1980. Boyd graduated from Snead State Jr. College, Jacksonville State University, and then Southwestern Baptist Theological Seminary in 1985. They worked in churches for ten years, including Boyd serving as associate pastor at First Baptist Atlanta with Dr. Charles Stanley and his son, Andy. The Stanleys gave Boyd the opportunity to write for some of their published books and taught Boyd and Rita lifelong lessons about servant leadership, loving people, prayer, and teaching the Bible.

In 1995, Boyd and Rita opened the Crown Ministries office in Atlanta and helped churches disciple their members in wise financial principles. The ministry grew significantly, and Boyd was eventually asked to serve as the national field director over 32 offices across the country. Soon after 9/11, with four teenage daughters at home, Boyd and Rita cofounded Ministry Ventures, where they trained and coached ministry leaders in the best practices of prayer, board development, strategy, administration, and fundraising. For 14 years they helped more than 1,000 ministries become their best.

Wisdom Hunters is another ministry God birthed in 2004 to help people "apply unchanging truth in a changing world" through sound biblical teaching and application. More than 250,000 daily readers in 86 countries are reached through email, social media, an app, a blog, audio, a podcast, and YouVersion. By God's grace, ten books have been self-published and eight books have been published with Harvest House, including *Learning to Lead Like Jesus.* Boyd likes to say, "I am not a great writer, but I am able to write about great things!"

Boyd and Rita serve on numerous boards, including Ministry Ventures, Wisdom Hunters, Souly Business, and The River Foundation. Rita serves on the helloHope board and is deeply involved in Spiritual Formations. They both love traveling, hiking, and loving on the grandbabies. Since 2016, Boyd has served as the president of the National Christian

Foundation of Georgia, helping 1,100 families manage donor-advised funds with over $40 million given annually to Christian causes.

They have four daughters, four sons-in-law, and eleven grandbabies. Boyd and Rita are most grateful to Jesus Christ for His love, forgiveness, and intimate relationship that gives them the courage, energy, and love to wake up every day to serve and love people. Fun fact: Rita recently served in the Amazon jungle, loving on children through medicine and vacation Bible school, while Boyd sailed in the British Virgin Islands!

WISDOM HUNTERS

*He who walks with wise men will be wise,
but the companion of fools will suffer harm.*

<small>Proverbs 13:20 nasb</small>

In 2003, Boyd Bailey began to informally email personal reflections from his morning devotional time to a select group of fellow wisdom hunters. Over time, these informal emails grew into Wisdom Hunters Daily Devotional. Today, thanks to God's favor and faithful followers, these emails and social media posts reach more than 150,000 readers each day.

Boyd remains relentless in the pursuit of wisdom and continues to daily write raw, original, real-time reflections from his personal encounters with the Lord.

Visit www.WisdomHunters.com where you can:

- Subscribe to free daily devotional emails

- Find out how to access our blog, Facebook, Twitter, Instagram, and the new Wisdom Hunters podcast

- Choose from a wide selection of devotional books on marriage, wisdom, wise living, and money, with books also for graduates, fathers, mothers, and more (ebook and print versions available)

- Download the free Wisdom Hunters app for Apple and Android

The thoughtful comments and wisdom followers share each day can help us all in our journeys with God.

National Christian
FOUNDATION®

Founded in 1982 and based in Atlanta, Georgia, the National Christian Foundation (NCF) is a charitable giving ministry that provides wise giving solutions, mobilizes resources, and inspires biblical generosity for Christian families, advisors, and charities. NCF is currently the ninth-largest US nonprofit, having accepted more than $9 billion in contributions. It has granted more than $7 billion to more than 40,000 charities. The NCF Giving Fund, or donor-advised fund, allows donors to make charitable contributions and then recommend grants to the charities they care about, over time. NCF is also an industry leader in accepting gifts of appreciated assets, such as stocks, real estate, and business interests, which enables donors to save on taxes and align their charitable goals with their family, business, estate, and legacy plans.

Learn more about NCF at www.NCFgiving.com.

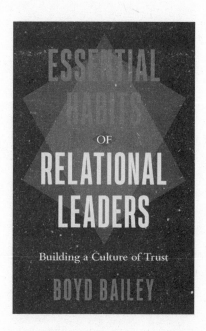

Become a Great Leader by Investing in Others

The strongest leaders are set apart by their relationships with their colleagues, their families, and the members of their community. They form bonds built on respect and mutual appreciation, and in doing so, they bring out the best in themselves and in others.

Improving as a relational leader is as easy as adding a few new tools to your belt while sharpening skills you already have. Best-selling author and ministry coach Boyd Bailey identifies 30 habits that will help you promote a culture of trust, love, and service wherever you lead. Grow in your ability to...

- cultivate God's heart toward people, recognizing their unique value as individuals
- prioritize love above all else, even over your own interests
- continually strive for personal growth, especially in your capacity for grace, selflessness, and emotional maturity

You'll find you are the most successful when you're helping those around you shine. By making these habits your own, you will grow into the kind of leader people can't wait to follow.

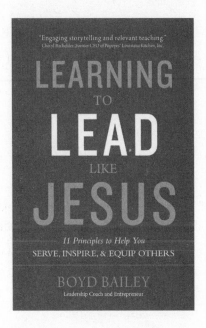

LEARNING TO LEAD LIKE JESUS

11 Principles to Help You
SERVE, INSPIRE, & EQUIP OTHERS

BOYD BAILEY
Leadership Coach and Entrepreneur

Have You Ever Met a Great Leader?

It's incredible when someone uses their gifts to make you feel valued and inspire you to greatness. What does it take to develop that kind of heart and influence? How can you become a leader like Jesus?

Join Boyd Bailey as he shows you how to mirror Jesus's heart and make a positive difference in those around you. Explore 11 common traits that mark successful leaders and learn the keys to growth in wisdom and humility. Through practical teaching, you will find that great leadership begins when you turn your focus to God and model Him in your attitude, conversations, and actions.

A faithful life and humble spirit make you a leader worth following. When you lean into the Lord and learn from His example of perfect leadership, you will see lives transformed—beginning with your own!

To learn more about Harvest House books and
to read sample chapters, visit our website:

www.harvesthousepublishers.com

HARVEST HOUSE PUBLISHERS
EUGENE, OREGON